The Law and the Dangerous Criminal

The Dangerous Offender Project

JUSTICE

John P. Conrad and Simon Dinitz
Project Co-Directors
The Academy for Contemporary Problems

The Law and the Dangerous Criminal

Statutory Attempts at
Definition and Control

Linda Sleffel

Lexington Books
D.C. Heath and Company
Lexington, Massachusetts
Toronto

Cover: Cuneiform characters for the word JUSTICE, the emblem of the Dangerous Offender Project.

Library of Congress Cataloging in Publication Data

Sleffel, Linda.
 The law and the dangerous criminal.

 1. Recidivists—United States—States. 2. Insane, Criminal and dangerous—United States—States. 3. Imprisonment—United States—States. 4. Preventive detention—United States—States. I. Title.
KF9226.Z95S57   345.73'03   77-287
ISBN 0-669-01481-8

Published simultaneously in Canada.

Printed in the United States of America.

International Standard Book Number: 0-669-01481-8

Library of Congress Catalog Card Number: 77-287

To my parents,
Merle and Zelma Sleffel

Contents

List of Tables

Foreword

Some offenders are more dangerous than others. This proposition is evident from any review of the population of any prison. The man who kills a group of nurses for no reason he can explain or a psychologist can infer is clearly more dangerous to the lives of others than is the ordinary thief in prison or the ordinary citizen outside. Because of the bizarre quality of the crime he committed, his case is known far and wide and will be remembered when lesser crimes have been long forgotten.

It would be an unfair and untrue exaggeration to imply that our prisons are full of dangerous people. They are not. But there are enough violent men and women incarcerated in them to require the peculiarly oppressive quality of control that characterizes the fortress-prison. The high walls and the concertina wire coiled on the top of perimeter fences would not be needed if all the prisons had to confine were thieves and confidence men. Heavily armed guards are not required for the control of people who are not dangerous.

There is indeed a quality we can call dangerousness that can be found in greater degree in some human beings than in others. It is a potential for doing great physical harm to others. Its origins are diverse: some subcultures encourage it as an aspect of manhood; some parents nurture it by inflicting violence on their offspring; and occasionally dangerousness is rooted in physiological abnormalities.

Whatever its origins, dangerousness presents formidable problems to the criminal justice system. Except for the clearly paranoid, no citizen can be restrained because of a potential for dangerousness. Once the potential has become manifest in an act, the offender can be punished, and the severity of the sanction imposed may take into account the opinion that the nature of the crime justifies the estimate that he may commit it again. Such an estimate violates a strict adherence to the principle that offenders are to be punished for what they have done, not for what they might do. The administration of our criminal law has never been scrupulous in its observance of this fine point, nor is it evident that the public would require that it should be. On the contrary, as this survey will show, public concern about violent crime has caused legislators to create a law of dangerousness. This body of statutes attempts to impose controls that exceed the stringency of the criminal law in spite of our inability to construct an empirically verifiable theory of dangerousness.

So far, our ability to detect this quality has depended on hindsight. A person is considered to be dangerous because he has performed acts that show him to be dangerous. Even this principle has been repeatedly shown to be fallacious.[1] Our legislators and our courts act on it anyway; no more tenable principle for the control of the dangerous offender has been discovered. Social scientists have never been able to isolate qualities existing in people defined as dangerous that enable us to predict that anyone who has not previously committed a violent act is certainly dangerous or even probably dangerous. Our skills at classification are so inadequate that we cannot say for sure that any particular person who in the past has been violent—or repeatedly violent—will commit such an act again if given the opportunity.

There are reasons to believe that we shall never have such predictive powers. We predict best when the event to be predicted is the outcome of a process we understand. We understand the process by which dynamite explodes and can predict its detonation accurately, thereby enabling us to protect ourselves from that kind of danger. But there are no well-understood processes which lead surely, or even with acceptable probability, to an act of violence. An act of interpersonal violence is not an event emerging from a process that can be understood as a chain of causes and effects. All we can say is that some people are more dangerous than others, but not all dangerous people explode into violence.

This is a conceptual blank that is not likely to be filled, but it is unthinkable that truly dangerous persons can be allowed to enjoy unrestrained freedom. Dangerousness probably cannot be defined rigorously, and we shall probably never have a test for determining whether an offender's dangerousness is extinguished. Nevertheless, society will continue to confront the criminal justice system with the demand that persons who have inflicted death or grave physical injury should be kept in custody until there is reason to believe that the danger they once presented has been surely reduced. This is a quandary from which social science cannot extricate the law; there can be no certainty in these matters.

In times past, most countries have relied on capital punishment to provide this assurance. Civilized men and women, however, have lost their taste for calling on the state to do in their behalf, as a clause in the social contract, what they would not as individuals be willing to do themselves. In spite of the resurgent calls for legislation to authorize capital punishment, the decline in its use during the years before its suspension attests to its irrelevance as an instrument of social control on which society will rely seriously. Because few of us wish to kill others for any reason, capital punishment remains in the statutes for the expression of outrage but not for the control of violent people.

We have to rely on the prison for the disposition of those we conceive to be dangerous. The civil disabilities that a prisoner suffers when he goes into custody are subject to restoration upon his release. Not only must society find a fair way to assess the hazards which justify this severe control, but it must also discover a rationale for determining when this vague quality of dangerousness has been sufficiently reduced to warrant a prisoner's restoration to the community.

The control of the dangerous offender is one of the tasks—in many eyes the most important task—assigned to the criminal justice system. Formerly the moral issue presented by science's inability to identify a person as dangerous could be disregarded. Retributive justice provided the desired protection either by the death penalty or through the protracted incarceration appropriate to an offender whose crimes were of the highest order of seriousness. For the retributivist who scales penalties by the gravity of the offense, the issue of control is incidental. Our laws have always been grounded on the objective of retribution. The difficulty that legislators have always encountered in assigning appropriate penalties has been eased by the implicit consideration that punitive incarceration also provides society with control of some offenders for whom it is required. The prisoner serving a life sentence for first-degree murder is thereby incapacitated as well as punished. We do not seriously concern ourselves in such cases with the need for incapacitation. Whether the prisoner is dangerous or not, he will be incapacitated indefinitely. It is when the sanctions are less severe that the justification for control becomes a true dilemma.

In spite of the sanctions that the criminal law has always provided, in spite of the flexibility by which they can be made more severe, the concern of the Anglo-American law during the last century has been to find ways of increasing even further the protection that the common law has always afforded. Legislation to provide for preventive detention of habitual criminals has been repealed only recently in England, after many years of ineffective and capricious use.[a] In the United States, public anxiety about particularly alarming or repellent offenses has inspired similar legislation. In this survey a wide assortment of statutes from all U.S. jurisdictions is under review. Some of these laws are concerned with the habitual criminal, usually defined as an offender who is proved to have committed on successive occasions any of a class of crimes including both dangerous and nondangerous offenses. Others provide for special incarcerative measures to be provided for sex offenders under the color of psychiatric treatment. Still others isolate other classes of offenders for special measures. All these laws have in common the focus on the offender rather than the offense. The assumption underlying each statute is that in the commission of his offense and the compilation of his record, the individual has established his dangerousness. Because of his status rather than because of his crime, the law is to treat him differently from an individual committing the same crime but not assigned a special status.

The Dangerous Offender Project is engaged in studies of the management of the repetitively violent offender. The primary points of reference are the criteria of fairness and effectiveness. The study will review the laws, assess the kinds of treatment available, document the measures of control, and determine what

[a]Preventive detention of repetitive offenders allowed for sentences to be imposed on such persons ranging up to fourteen years, to be served in specialized prisons restricted to detainees. This provision of the English penal law was abolished in the Criminal Justice Act of 1967.

impact the present system has on the individuals with whom it is concerned and what if any improvements may be available from the existing fund of knowledge. It will make an intensive assessment of the proportion of violent crime for which repetitively violent offenders are responsible, and it will examine the measures taken by the courts to use existing laws in disposing of charges against them. This inventory of dangerous offender legislation is the first of a series of studies that will be published by Lexington Books in an examination of society's contention with this formidable problem.

This review is primarily concerned with the fairness of this class of legislation. The criterion is slippery; fairness can hardly be measured and the comparisons that can be made among the laws considered are without the benefit of data regarding their use. Some points of importance to keep in mind should be formulated here, however.

First, however fairness is defined, the verification of its observance presents a different problem when one is considering a law that punishes the offender for his offense from that presented by a law that restrains him because of his status. When someone is to be punished for an act, he can require that proof be made in open court that the act took place and that he did it. That proof under legal procedures can be conclusively established; everything done in court is directed to proving guilt beyond a reasonable doubt.

Where someone is to be restrained because of his status, the premise of the case against him is not that he performed some punishable act but rather that his performance of that act justifies the prediction that he will do it again. The assumption that such a prediction can be validly made distorts the law. The common law requires the maximum proof possible that A did B. It will not settle for some degree of probability. But the law of dangerousness is quite willing to compromise on this point. It will settle for probability as its criterion for custodial control, ordinarily protracted far beyond the usual sanctions of the criminal law. It will also allow for such control to be imposed for a degree of probability which scarcely exceeds mere chance.[2] It is not easy to reconcile this statistical basis for restraint with the criteria for fairness which the common law imposes on the criminal court. The courts' reluctance to use habitual criminal statutes surely reflects the sense of unfairness perceived in sentencing by class rather than by offense. If the prediction of dangerousness has to be made, most courts seem content to leave it to parole boards, which can decide for themselves how much risk each offender appearing before them may present. We have no way of testing the predictions that parole boards make on the basis of which offenders are kept in prison, but obviously such decisions have the full incapacitating effect of the kinds of dangerous offender legislation under review in this book. We are left with the conclusion that there is no way in which the criminal law can restrain an offender because of a prediction of dangerousness that will satisfy our standard of fairness.

A second objection on the score of unfairness arises from the vagueness and even the tautologies that characterize most such legislation. The precision of language on which the law usually insists degenerates into mere floundering with verbiage and concepts. Laws which prescribe that a dangerous offender is anyone whose pattern of offenses demonstrate that he is a danger to others can have been written and passed only in the white heat of outrage concerning an apparent crime wave, without the consideration of whether and how they might be applied by cooler heads. We believe that we have exposed a serious need for a legislative housecleaning of statutes which have never served any purpose but the satisfaction of public clamor. A sense of fastidiousness should dictate their removal from the codes which they disfigure.

We have been unable to test the law of dangerousness by comparing its actual use with potential use. It would be a valuable but difficult exercise to determine what percentage of repetitive offenders eligible for confinement as habitual criminals or sexual psychopaths actually were subjected to such sanctions. Such a study could shed light on the value of such legislation in the incapacitation of supposedly dangerous offenders by comparing the careers of comparable offenders given conventional sentences with those receiving special sentences for dangerousness. This investigation must come under the heading of research that should be done; it has not been within our means or scope to do it.

For the present, the evidence assembled in this review indicates clearly that public fear and anger have deflected Anglo-American criminal law from its consistently strict emphasis on punishment for violation of the law rather than assignment to a status. Because of the vagueness with which these laws have been written and because of their optional use, they are seen to be unfair, and this perception leads to an ineffective application. It is a vicious circle made more vicious by the obvious potentiality of such laws for leverage in plea-bargaining.

Finally, most offenders who are eligible for sentencing as dangerous are poor and too often black or brown. The application of our criminal laws is far too vulnerable to the charge that it is class-oriented and oppressive. We shall do well to remove from the statutes this redundant legislation that unnecessarily exposes the courts to charges of prejudice in the administration of justice.

Although we are convinced that there should not be a law of dangerousness and that the disorganized pieces of bad legislation under review here do not constitute a coherent public policy, we are far from taking the position that nothing can or should be done to improve the control of the offenders who are repetitively violent. The content of a sound public policy in these matters is the focus of the Dangerous Offender Project. In future publications we expect to contribute to models for optimal control by the criminal justice system. In this volume our contribution is essentially negative: the laws we have create many needless problems in the administration of criminal justice, and they solve no problems at all.

John P. Conrad

Notes

1. For a critical review of the literature on the prediction of dangerousness, see Norval Morris, *The Future of Imprisonment* (Chicago: University of Chicago Press, 1974), pp. 62-73.

2. Ibid., pp. 67-71.

Introduction

This book is a survey of state statutes applicable to dangerous offenders; it was undertaken as part of a larger project concerned generally with the possibilities for the identification and control of the dangerous offender. Under a working definition adopted by the project, a dangerous offender is anyone who repetitively commits violent offenses.

It is difficult to define the term "violent offense," since an offense like robbery creates a great risk of harm although it may be carried out with no physical injury to the victim. But "violent offense" will be used generally to refer to offenses that cause physical injury or that, like robbery, create immediate, direct risk of injury. The term "serious offense" will be used to refer to crimes that are not violent but sufficiently troublesome to society to warrant relatively severe penalties. Examples would be extortion and large-scale fraud.

A clear picture of the present state of statutory law is necessary if better laws for controlling violent offenders are to be written; it is the purpose of this survey to provide that picture. The research was directed toward discovering as many as possible of the statutes in every state that could apply to violent offenders. It is intended to serve as a starting point for legislators and criminal justice planners in considering changes in the law. (The survey covers the fifty states, the federal government, the District of Columbia, and Puerto Rico.)

What this book will indicate most clearly is that there is no organized statutory approach to the problem posed by the dangerous offender. Instead, state codes include a miscellaneous collection of statutes that single out for special attention groups that include both violent and nonviolent offenders.

Some statutes were written with the specific purpose of controlling dangerous offenders; others have different purposes and apply incidentally to violent offenders. Very few apply only to violent offenders.

Nevertheless, some statutes can be selected as being more applicable to violent offenders than other laws. These statutes illustrate special concerns of legislatures and the public with respect to crime, and they provide some idea of what kinds of offenders are considered dangerous by the public.

Several types of statutes have been selected for inclusion in this survey. Habitual criminal laws and sexual psychopath laws are the two most obvious. Although habitual criminal laws have fallen into disuse in many states, they represent the traditional approach for incapacitating repetitive offenders, including, of course, both violent and nonviolent offenders. Sexual psychopath laws probably remain largely unused as well; however, they illustrate the medical model for both the selection and the treatment of dangerous offenders. Their complex and detailed nature shows the extent of preoccupation with the special threat that sex offenders have been thought to pose. Sexual psychopath laws also are concerned with two elements of overriding importance in much of the thinking about dangerous offenders. One is mental abnormality, which is closely associated with dangerousness both in the public mind and in statutory and case law. The other is the prediction of violent behavior, or other criminal behavior, which is of course a point of great concern and difficulty in dealing with dangerous offenders.

In addition, the survey includes legislation dealing with incompetence to stand trial and disposition after acquittal by reason of insanity. Not only do these provisions raise again the question of the association between mental abnormality and dangerousness, but both have been used at times for the long-term incapacitation of persons who were thought to be dangerous but who could not be reached by the usual criminal process.

Civil commitment procedures are not included, since most civilly committed patients will not have entered the criminal process formally, and since it may be presumed that civil commitment would rarely be chosen as a means of dealing with persons who have committed the kind of violent offenses that are the concern of this project.

The study includes procedures for transferring prisoners from correctional to mental institutions, since this is another method of incapacitating persons thought to be particularly dangerous. It has been used on occasion to confine persons who have served their sentences and therefore can no longer be kept in custody under criminal laws.

Selected sentencing provisions are included on the assumption that they reveal legislative thinking about what kinds of offenders pose special dangers to public safety. Such statutes may be of special interest now that mandatory sentences are being proposed as appropriate and effective means of dealing with such classes of criminals as drug offenders and those who use firearms in their crimes.

Also included is a group of statutes that define classes of offenders such as "dangerous offender," "repeat offender," and "sex offender." Some of these definitions have legal consequences such as special security, registration requirements, or ineligibility for parole. Others involve no change in disposition but again may reveal legislative thinking on dangerousness.

The first task is to list and describe the statutes, and to classify them so that comparisons among states can be made. The second is to analyze them, considering the following practical, constitutional, and ethical questions: Do the statutes accomplish their purpose? Do they provide different handling for violent offenders than for other offenders? Does this special handling offer useful and efficient means for controlling violent offenders? Is the special treatment necessary? How does it comport with constitutional standards? Is it ethically acceptable as a means of punishing offenders or protecting society?

This analysis will show that the statutes are lacking in a number of respects. Most of them do not appear to be particularly useful in controlling violent offenders. A number of them raise serious constitutional questions. Their cost in both human rights and public resources often seems greatly to outweigh their benefits. Therefore some guidelines and proposals will be offered for drafting better statutes.

A number of special problems attend legal research in this area. The statutes surveyed are scattered throughout state codes. Although a careful search of the statutes of each state was made, it is likely that some statutes of interest to the survey were not discovered.

Another difficulty arises from the fact that the survey involves an area of the law that is presently of intense public interest and is therefore the subject of much legislative scrutiny and revision. The many changes being made in state statutes mean that any compilation will become rapidly outdated. This publication will attempt to be accurate in representing the state of the law on December 31, 1975.

Because of the volume of litigation on several issues of major importance to this study, constitutional standards are shifting rapidly. Therefore the discussions of constitutional issues will suggest some trends that may be followed in future cases.

At a time when numerous kinds of statutory changes are being proposed as solutions to rising crime rates, it is important to know exactly what the statutes are at present, and to consider how statutory revisions can provide more efficient means for dealing with crime. This book is written in the hope that it can help to provide the necessary background for thoughtful consideration of better criminal laws.

Acknowledgments

Research for this book was done under a grant from Lilly Endowment, Indianapolis, to the Dangerous Offender Project of the Academy for Contemporary Problems, Columbus, Ohio. To John P. Conrad and Simon Dinitz, co-directors of the project, I am grateful for assistance and guidance in the research and writing. Much of the research on state statutes was done by Sally Sickles and June Perin, who demonstrated great care and persistence in a difficult task. Other members of the project staff provided valuable advice and comments during the course of my work. I owe a great debt to Lois G. Gaber and Sherry Flannery for their careful and patient typing of the manuscript. Professor Vincent Nathan of the University of Toledo College of Law, and Herbert Edelhertz of Battelle-Seattle, Human Affairs Research Center, generously granted their time to review the draft and offer comments and suggestions. To these people, to the many friends who offered support and encouragement, and to my husband, Dan Moore, who exhibited truly admirable patience during the course of the work, I am deeply grateful. I, of course, am responsible for any errors or omissions in this book.

1

Habitual Criminal Statutes

Introduction

Habitual criminal laws are important to a consideration of legal handling of violent offenders because they are the oldest and most traditional method used in the United States for singling out for special handling offenders thought to pose unusual threats to society. They have been on the books in most states since early in this century, and they have been regarded as a logical and effective means of dealing with repeat offenders, especially those who commit serious crimes. This chapter is intended to give a clear and complete picture of what crimes the statutes cover, how they operate, and whether they accomplish the job they are intended to do.

This chapter includes all statutes that provide for imposing an increased penalty based on proof of previous convictions. In addition to these general statutes, many states also provide for augmented penalties for the repetition of specific offenses, for example, robbery with a gun. Such laws are also relevant to this study, but they are not included because compilation would require an amount of research disproportionate to its value.

The problem of recidivists arose after nineteenth-century British penal reforms eliminated hanging for minor offenses. Repeal of such harsh penalties led to the emergence of a new category of criminal, the repeat offender, and laws to deal with him developed concurrently with the reform movement. The concept of preventive detention for repeat offenders was first suggested by the Gladstone Committee Report of 1895.[1] The first rationale for imposing long sentences on recidivists was simply to incapacitate them; early proposals for British habitual criminal laws envisioned less onerous conditions of confinement for such prisoners.[2] The rationales of deterrence and rehabilitation soon entered the picture, however, and they have influenced the law up to present times.

The earliest U.S. recidivist statutes provided increased penalties only for repetition of the same offense. Most present statutes impose added penalties for repetition of any of a broad class of offenses. The U.S. movement to pass habitual criminal laws was given impetus by the widely publicized enactment of the *Baumes Laws* in New York in 1926.[3] Having withstood numerous constitutional challenges, recidivist laws are now in effect in forty-three U.S. jurisdictions. (Eight states have no habitual criminal statutes: Illinois, Maryland, Massachusetts, Mississippi, Ohio, Pennsylvania, Utah, and Virginia.)

This survey divides habitual criminal laws into two main categories. The

1

more traditional type allows imposition of a long sentence, or even a life sentence, upon conviction on the present charge and proof of previous convictions. Forty jurisdictions have some version of this kind of habitual criminal law.[4] The second variety, the Model Penal Code approach, requires a separate determination involving the defendant's character, mental condition, and propensities for future offenses. Five such statutes are in effect, the best known being the federal provisions for sentencing of "dangerous special offenders," 18 U.S.C. 3575.

General Characteristics of Traditional Statutes

The traditional habitual criminal statutes provide for added penalties that are imposed upon conviction on the present charge and proof of the required number of previous convictions. A few states make life terms or very long terms mandatory upon proof of two or three previous felony convictions. A number of other states provide mandatory minimum terms for the third or fourth felony. Most habitual criminal laws leave imposition of penalties to the discretion of the sentencing court and give the court a wide range of authorized penalties from which to choose. Table 1-1 lists in detail the penalty structure of the traditional laws, which have been divided for this purpose into seventy-nine separate penalty provisions. Procedure for imposing the added penalties tends to be simple. In most states the prosecutor has total discretion to decide whether to invoke the habitual criminal statute. If he decides to do so, most states require that the defendant be charged as a habitual criminal in the indictment for the present offense, or in a separate indictment.

In seventeen states, authority to invoke the statute is specifically granted to the prosecutor, or the requirement of an indictment or information places it within his general powers. In eight states the statute is invoked by the prosecutor with court approval, or by the court on its own motion. In two states the statute is brought into play by motion of the prosecutor. In twelve states the statutes do not specify how they are to be invoked.

Once the issue is properly pleaded, all that is required for imposition of the additional sentence is proof that the defendant is the same person as the one shown by court records to have been convicted of the previous crimes. In three states (Connecticut, Minnesota, and New York) the statute requires an additional finding by the trial court that the defendant has propensities toward the commission of further offenses, or that an extended sentence is in the public interest (see table 1-1). Convictions that would have been invalid under due process requirements with retroactive effect, such as the right of indigents to appointed counsel, cannot be considered in proving the necessary record of previous offenses. In addition, most habitual criminal statutes provide that to be counted as separate previous offenses, the crimes must not have been committed as part of one criminal transaction.[a]

Several states impose an additional requirement that the defendant have actually served a prison term for the previous offenses. This requirement is included in thirteen of the seventy-nine penalty provisions listed in table 1-1.

A number of states provide that the trier of fact may not be informed of the habitual criminal charge until after the defendant is found guilty on the present charge; this eliminates the possible prejudicial effect of the previous record.

Once the previous convictions have been proved, the court either will impose a mandatory sentence or will exercise its general sentencing authority and select a sentence from those authorized.

In three jurisdictions, provisions for sentencing recidivists may be characterized simply as part of the general scheme of sentencing, rather than as separate habitual criminal statutes. The Kansas provisions are found with other sentencing statutes, and no procedure is established by statute, except invocation of the statute by motion of the prosecutor. Similarly, the District of Columbia and Puerto Rico statutes include no procedure but simply grant authority for imposing the longer sentences on defendants with the required record of previous convictions.

Offenses Covered

As might be expected, very few recidivist statutes attempt to distinguish violent offenders from other offenders. Most of the statutes apply to any felony; several apply to at least some misdemeanors, and a handful apply to any criminal offense. Table 1-2 illustrates the offenses covered by the seventy-nine provisions shown in table 1-1.

Even among these limited groups of violent offenses, we find a few that are not violent: sodomy is included in the Delaware statute; burglary and safecracking are included in the South Carolina statute; and abduction of a female from her parents and Schedule I drug offenses are listed in the Tennessee statute. Arguably, some others—such as attempts at assault, arson, or kidnaping—might not be considered violent.

---

[a]E.g., "Any person, who, after having been convicted within this state of a felony, or who, after having been convicted under the laws of any other state or the United States or any foreign government of a crime which if committed in this state would be a felony, thereafter commits any subsequent felony within this state...." (West's La. Stat. Ann. 15:529.1); "An offender who has been previously convicted of a felony and the present offense is a second felony committed on a different occasion that the first...." (Rev. Codes Mont. Ann. 95-1507).

Table 1-1
Sentencing Structure under Traditional Habitual Criminal Statutes

State	Present Offense	Number of Previous Offenses	Previous Offense
Alabama	—	1	same offense
Alaska	felony	1	felony
	felony	2	felonies
	felony	3	felonies
	petty larceny, misdemeanor with element of fraud	3	burglary, certain larcenies
Arkansas	felony	1	felony
	murder, rape, carnal abuse, kidnaping	2	murder, rape, carnal abuse, kidnaping
Arizona	any crime	1	petty theft, molesting a child under 16, contributing to delinquency of minor, offense involving lewd and lascivious conduct, or any felony
California	robbery, first-degree burglary, burglary with explosives, rape with force or violence, arson, murder, assault with intent to commit murder, train wrecking, felonious assault with a deadly weapon, extortion, kidnaping, escape from a state prison by use of force or dangerous or deadly weapons, rape or fornication or sodomy or carnal abuse of a child under 14, lewd or lascivious act with a child, or conspiracy to commit any of the above.	2	robbery, burglary, burglary with explosives, rape with force or violence, arson, murder, assault with intent to commit murder, grand theft, bribery of a public official, perjury, subornation of perjury, train wrecking, feloniously receiving stolen goods, felonious assault with a deadly weapon, extortion, kidnaping, mayhem, escape from a state prison, rape or fornication or sodomy or carnal abuse of a child under the age of 14 years, lewd and lascivious act with a child, or conspiracy to commit any of the above.
Colorado	felony	2	felonies
	felony	3	felonies

Previous[a] Sentence	Required Penalty[b]	Allowed Penalty
—	sentence must be at least 1/4 longer than first sentence, unless this would exceed maximum	
—	not less than minimum for offense	up to twice maximum for offense
—	not less than minimum	up to twice maximum for second offense
—	20 years	up to life
—	1 year	—
—	life (not clear whether required or allowed)	
—	life (or death, if prescribed for offense)	—
—	if normal penalty is less than 5, then not more than 10; if normal penalty is more than 5, then not less than 10	—
terms served	life sentence (court has discretion to reverse finding that defendant is habitual criminal within 60 days. If it does, the life term is not imposed).	—
—	not less than maximum for offense	up to 3 times maximum
—	life	—

Table 1-1 (cont.)

State	Present Offense	Number of Previous Offenses	Previous Offense
Connecticut	misdemeanor theft	1	misdemeanor theft
	3rd- or 4th-degree larceny	2	larceny
	felony	1	felony
	felony	1	felony
	manslaughter, arson, rape, kidnaping, first- or second-degree robbery, first-degree assault	1	manslaughter, arson, rape, first- or second-degree robbery, first-degree assault, murder, kidnaping attempt at any of the above
Delaware	felony	3	felony
	first and second degree murder, first-degree arson, first- or second-degree burglary, kidnaping, first-degree assault, first-degree robbery, rape, sodomy	2	first or second degree murder, first-degree arson, first or second degree burglary, kidnaping, first-degree assault, first-degree robbery, rape, sodomy
Florida	felony or attempted felony	1	felony or attempted felony
	felony or attempted felony	3	felony or attempted felony
Georgia	felony	3	felonies
Idaho	felony	2	felonies
Indiana	felony	2	felonies
Iowa	petty larceny (persons over 18)	3	petty larceny
	felony	2	felonies
	burglary, robbery, counterfeiting, forgery, larceny over $20, breaking & entering with intent to commit public offense	2	burglary, robbery, forgery, larceny over $20, breaking & entering with intent to commit public offense and counterfeiting
Kansas	felony	1	felony

Previous[a] Sentence	Required Penalty[b]	Allowed Penalty
—	—	up to 3 years
—	—	up to 5 years if court finds in public interest
term in state prison	—	up to twice maximum for current offense
sentence of 1 year to life	—	sentence for next more serious felony if court finds longer sentence in public interest
sentence of 1 year to life	—	life, if court finds it in public interest
—	—	life
—	life term	—
—	maximum for offense	up to twice maximum
—	life	—
—	must serve maximum set by judge or jury	—
—	not less than 5	up to life
time served	life term	—
—	up to 3 years	—
commitment to prison on sentence of 3 or more	—	up to 25 years
—	—	up to 40 years
—	—	indeterminate sentence with minimum not less than least minimum nor more than twice greatest minimum for offense and

Table 1-1 (cont.)

State	Present Offense	Number of Previous Offenses	Previous Offense
Kansas (cont.)			
	felony	2	felonies
Kentucky	Class A felony	2	felonies
	Class B felony	2	felonies
	Class C or D felony ·	2	felonies
Louisiana	felony	1	felony
	felony	2	felonies
	felony	3	felonies
Maine	felony	1	felony
Michigan	felony	1	felony
	felony	2	felonies
Minnesota	felony	1	felony within last 10 years
Missouri	felony	1	felony or attempted felony

Previous[a] Sentence	Required Penalty[b]	Allowed Penalty
		maximum of not less than regular maximum nor more than twice regular maximum
–	–	indeterminate sentence with minimum not less than least minimum nor more than three times greatest minimum for offense and maximum of not less than regular maximum nor more than life.
imprison- ment on sentences of one year or more	–	indeterminate term with maximum of life
imprison- ment on sentences of one year or more	–	indeterminate term with maximum of not less than 20 years nor more than life.
imprison- ment on sentences of one year or more	–	indeterminate term with maximum of not less than 10 years nor more than 20.
–	1/3 of maximum for offense	up to twice maximum
–	1/2 of maximum for offense	up to twice maximum
–	maximum for offense; not less than 20	up to life
–	–	any term of years
–	–	–if penalty is less than life, then any sentence from probation to 1-1/2 times maximum–if penalty is life, then any term up to life.
–	–	–if penalty is less than life, up to twice maximum–if penalty is life, up to life term
–	–	maximum for offense multiplied by number of previous convictions; not to exceed 40 years (requires trial court finding that defendant has propensity for future crimes of violence)
–	defendant will be designated as habitual criminal, but no penalties listed	

Table 1-1 (cont.)

State	Present Offense	Number of Previous Offenses	Previous Offense
Montana	felony	1	felony
Nebraska	felony	2	felonies
New Jersey	misdemeanor or high misdemeanor	1	high misdemeanor
	misdemeanor or high misdemeanor	2	high misdemeanor
	misdemeanor or high misdemeanor	3	high misdemeanor
	(no penalties cited for felony repeaters)		
New Mexico	felony	1	felony
	felony	2	felonies
	felony	3	felonies
New York	felony	2	felonies
Nevada	felony, petty larceny or any crime with element of fraud or intent to defraud	2 3	felonies *or* petty larcenies or misde-meanors or gross misdemean-ors with element of fraud or intent to defraud
	felony, petty larceny or any crime with element of fraud or intent to defraud	3 5	felonies *or* petty larcenies or misde-meanors or gross misdemean-ors with element of fraud or intent to defraud
North Carolina	felony	2	felonies
Oklahoma	petty larceny, attempted felony	1	felony
	felony	1	felony

Previous[a] Sentence	Required Penalty[b]	Allowed Penalty
—	at least 5 years	up to 100 years
commitment on sentence of 1 year or more	10 years	up to 60 years; if longer sentence is provided for offense it prevails
—	—	up to twice maximum for offense
—	—	up to 3 times maximum for offense
—	—	any term up to life
—	half of maximum for offense	up to twice maximum
—	maximum for offense	up to 3 times maximum
—	life term	—
imprisonment on sentence of more than 1 year	—	sentence for Class A-1 felony; minimum 15-25, maximum life (requires finding by sentencing court that history & character of defendant & nature & circumstances of criminal conduct indicate that extended incarceration & lifetime supervision will best serve public interest)
—	10 years	up to 20 years
—	life term	—
—	20 years	up to life (calculated at 40 years for parole purposes) (Not eligible for parole until 75% of term served. Sentence cannot be suspended. Term cannot be reduced below 75% for good behavior or other reason.)
—	—	up to 5 years
—	if penalty is 5 or more, not less than 10	if penalty is 5 or less, up to 10 years

Table 1-1 (cont.)

State	Present Offense	Number of Previous Offenses	Previous Offense
Rhode Island	felony	2	felonies
South Carolina	murder, voluntary manslaughter, rape, armed robbery, highway robbery, assault with intent to ravish, bank robbery, arson, burglary, safe-cracking, attempt at any of above	3	same offenses
	same as above	4	same as above
South Dakota	felony	1	felony or attempted felony
	felony	3	felonies
Tennessee	capital crime, assault with intent to commit murder, malicious shooting or stabbing, assault with intent to commit rape, mayhem, abduction of female from parents or manufacturing, selling or delivering Schedule I drugs	2	same offenses
Texas	3rd-degree felony	1	felony
	2nd-degree felony	1	felony
	1st-degree felony	1	felony
	felony	2	felonies
Vermont	felony	3	felonies or attempted felonies
Washington	felony, petty larceny, misdemeanor or gross misdemeanor with element of fraud or intent to defraud	1	felony *or*
		2	petty larcenies, misdemeanor or gross misdemeanor with element of fraud or intent to defraud
	same as above	2	felonies *or*
		4	of above misdemeanors
West Virginia	felony	1	felony
Wisconsin	any offense	1	felony within 5-year period

Previous[a] Sentence	Required Penalty[b]	Allowed Penalty
with prison sentences	–	up to 25 in addition to present sentence (not eligible for parole until 5 of 25 served)
–	maximum for offense	–
–	life term	–
–	–	up to twice maximum for offense
–	–	life term
–	life term with no suspension, parole, or reduction for good behavior	–
–	sentence for 2nd-degree felony	–
–	sentence for 1st-degree felony	–
–	15 years	up to 99 years
–	life term	–
–	–	life term
–	not less than 10	sterilization
–	life term	sterilization
–	if penalty is definite term, 5 additional years; if indeterminate term, 5 added to maximum	–
–	–	if maximum is 1 year or less up to 3 years; if maximum 1-10 increase as much as 6; if maximum more than 10, increase as much as 10

Table 1-1 (cont.)

State	Present Offense	Number of Previous Offenses	Previous Offense
Wisconsin (cont.)	any offense	3	misdemeanors within 5-year period
Wyoming	felony	2	felonies
	felony	3	felonies
District of Columbia	any offense under D.C. law	1	same offense as presently charged
	any offense under D.C. law	2	same offense as presently charged
	felony	2	felonies punishable by terms of more than 2 years
Puerto Rico	petty larceny or attempt at crime punishable by imprisonment in penitentiary	1	same offenses
	any offense (except petty larceny or attempt at crime punishable by imprisonment in penitentiary)	1	petty larceny or attempt at offense punishable by imprisonment in penitentiary
	petty larceny or attempt at crime punishable by 5 years or less	1	offense punishable by imprisonment in penitentiary
	any offense (except petty larceny or attempt at crime punishable by 5 years or less	1	offense punishable by imprisonment in penitentiary
	felony	2	felonies

aThis column includes information on the requirement of a few state statutes that the defendant must have actually served a sentence for the previous offense in order for the enhanced penalty to be imposed.

bDifficulties arose in categorizing whether the penalty was required or allowed in habitual criminal statutes. Most sentencing statutes state that a trial court "shall" impose the author-

Previous[a] Sentence	Required Penalty[b]	Allowed Penalty
—	—	if maximum 1 year or less, up to 3 yrs, if maximum 1 or more, increase as much as 2
—	10 years	up to 50
—	life term	—
—	—	fine of 1 1/2 times regular fine and prison term of 1 1/2 times maximum for offense
—	—	fine of 3 times regular fine and prison term of 3 times maximum for offense
—	—	any term up to life, if court finds that such sentence will best serve public interest
—	—	up to 5 years
—	—	if penalty would be life in discretion of court, then life; if penalty would be less than life, then maximum for first offense
—	—	up to 5 years
—	—	if penalty is more than 5, then not less than 10; if 5 or less, then not more than 10
imprisonment in Puerto Rico for 5 or more years	15 years	—

ized sentence; nevertheless, usually the court has the power to suspend all or part of the sentence. Mandatory sentencing statutes, on the other hand, remove this discretion from the trial court. The column headed "Required Penalty" includes all sentences that the statute says the court "shall" impose. Also included are sentencing provisions that specify that no suspension is authorized. The column headed "Allowed Penalty" includes all sentences that the statute says the trial court "may" impose.

Table 1-2
Offenses Covered by Provisions Shown in Table 1-1

Type of Offense	Number of Provisions
Violent offenses	6
Serious felonies	3
All felonies	48
Misdemeanors (indicates that statute applies to at least some misdemeanors)	13
All offenses	7

The following provisions are included in the category of violent offenses above:

Arkansas—for murder, rape, carnal abuse, or kidnaping, with two previous convictions of any of the same offenses, a life term is required.

Connecticut—for manslaughter, arson, rape, kidnaping, first- or second-degree robbery, or first-degree assault, with one previous conviction of manslaughter, arson, rape, kidnaping, first- or second-degree assault, murder, or attempt at any of these, accompanied by a sentence of one year to life, the court has discretion to impose a life sentence, if it finds it in the public interest.

Delaware—for first- or second-degree murder, first-degree arson, first- or second-degree burglary, kidnaping, first-degree assault, first-degree robbery, rape, or sodomy, with two previous convictions of any of the same offenses, a life term is required.

South Carolina—for murder, voluntary manslaughter, rape, armed robbery, highway robbery, assault with intent to ravish, bank robbery, arson, burglary, safecracking, or attempt at any of these, with three previous convictions of any of the same offenses, the maximum sentence for the offense is required. If there are four previous convictions, a life term is required.

Tennessee—for a capital crime, assault with intent to commit murder, malicious shooting or stabbing, assault with intent to commit rape, mayhem, abduction of a female from her parents, or manufacturing, selling, or delivering Schedule I drugs, with two previous convictions of the same offenses, a life term is required, with no suspension, parole, or reduction for good behavior.

The requirement in thirteen provisions of having served a previous prison term, or a term of a specified length, in addition to the previous convictions, may limit application of the statute to more serious offenses, although not necessarily to violent offenses. (Only felonies are included in these thirteen provisions.)

The California statute, which applies only to present offenses involving violence or sexual abuse of children along with conspiracy to commit violent offenses, lists among previous offenses to be taken into account not only the same group of violent offenses, but also grand theft, bribery of a public official, perjury, subornation of perjury, and feloniously receiving stolen goods.

Most of the thirteen provisions that apply to misdemeanors are clearly directed toward the control of the chronic shoplifter or forger.[b] Most of these provisions apply only to theft offenses.

The New Jersey statute, the only one that applies to other misdemeanors, is also exceptional because it has three separate penalty provisions, all applying to misdemeanors or high misdemeanors, with different numbers of previous convictions, but there is no provision for sentencing repeat felony offenders.

The Washington statute imposes the harshest penalties for repeated misdemeanors. A defendant convicted of a felony, petty larceny, or a misdemeanor or gross misdemeanor with an element of fraud or intent to defraud, who also has previous convictions of one felony or two petty larcenies or misdemeanors or gross misdemeanors with an element of fraud or intent to defraud, must be sentenced to not less than ten years. If the previous record includes two felonies or four petty larcenies or misdemeanors or gross misdemeanors with an element of fraud or intent to defraud, a life term is required. In addition, a defendant falling into either category will be declared a habitual criminal, and Rev. Code Wash. Ann. 9.92.100 authorizes the sterilization of habitual criminals.

Penalties

With the exception of the misdemeanor recidivist provisions described above, the heaviest penalties (mandatory or discretionary life terms) are found in the provisions covering the most serious offenses (see table 1-3).

The sentences that do not involve life terms fall into three classes:

1. Approximately half of all statutes specify certain terms of years, with

Table 1-3
Life Terms

Type of Offense	Provisions with Required Life Terms[a]	Provisions with Discretionary Life Terms	Total Provisions
Violent offenses	4	1	6
Serious felonies	1	2	3
All felonies	8	18	48
Misdemeanors	1	1	13
All offenses	0	0	7

aThis category also includes terms of fifty years or more.

bE.g., Alaska, petty larceny or misdemeanor with element of fraud; Connecticut, misdemeanor theft or third- or fourth-degree larceny; Iowa, petty larceny; Washington, felony, petty larceny, or gross misdemeanor with element of fraud or intent to defraud.

widely varying lengths from state to state. For example, the Idaho statute provides that a defendant convicted of a felony who has two previous felony convictions must be sentenced to not less than five years. In North Carolina a felony offender with the same record must be sentenced to at least twenty years and could receive a life sentence.

2. Some sentences—about two-fifths—are related to the usual term for the offense in question. In Minnesota, a repeat felony offender may be sentenced to a term that is calculated by multiplying the maximum sentence for the offense by the number of previous offenses, with the sentence not to exceed forty years in any case. The New Mexico statute provides that a felony offender with one previous felony conviction must be sentenced to at least half the maximum term for the present offense, and may be sentenced to as much as twice the maximum. If the offender has two previous convictions, he must be sentenced to the maximum for the offense, and he may receive three times the maximum. (A life term is required for felony offenders with three previous felonies.) The New Jersey statute allows courts to impose the following sentences: for a misdemeanor or high misdemeanor with one previous high misdemeanor, up to twice the maximum for the present offense; with two previous high misdemeanors, up to three times the maximum for the present offense. (A life sentence is allowed if there are three previous high misdemeanors.)

3. A few states, whose criminal offenses are divided into several classes of seriousness, provide for repeat felony offenders to be sentenced for a more serious class of offense than the one on which they have just been convicted.

Clearly, the second and third kinds of sentence are more closely related to the seriousness of at least the present offense, but of course none of the three types relates the sentence imposed to the violent nature of either present or past offenses.

Usefulness

For a number of reasons, traditional habitual criminal statutes are of little use in singling out and dealing with the violent offender. First, few of the statutes now on the books make any attempt to distinguish between violent and nonviolent offenses. Most do not even distinguish between serious and trivial felonies. This means that the shoplifter or forger who commits as many as three or four offenses involving amounts barely within the felony theft category would be subject to the extended term as a habitual offender. In fact, some commentators suggest that habitual criminal statutes are applied more often to this category of offender than to those who commit very serious offenses. Daniel Katkin believes that persons sentenced under such laws tend to be habitual petty offenders. He reported that a survey of British prisoners under preventive confinement shows most to be thieves and "losers" in all spheres of life.[5] He suggested further that when such statutes are used as plea-bargaining tools against organized or professional criminals, they bring guilty pleas only for offenses that are not subject to long sentences. He concluded that if the habitual criminal laws were not available to be used in plea bargaining, more of these offenders would go to trial and receive long terms.[6]

The wide discretion allowed in deciding whether to invoke a habitual criminal statute decreases the likelihood that the statutes will be used consistently against persons who have committed serious offenses, much less against those who have committed violent offenses. Such discretion, coupled with the harshness of many of the sentences and especially of mandatory sentences, gives the prosecutor an extremely powerful weapon to use in plea-bargaining.

Discretion is a weapon that may be even more powerful in cases of minor offenses than in serious ones, since the defendant who has committed a serious offense has less to lose if he risks invoking the habitual criminal statute by going to trial. Although this study has not collected any data on the frequency of the use of such statutes, it seems reasonable to assume that in most jurisdictions they are more important in plea-bargaining than in actual application. (Conversations with prison wardens and prosecutors have indicated that the number of defendants prosecuted and sentenced under the statutes is small, but they are used much more frequently in plea-bargaining.)

Certain factors that may be characterized as largely coincidental can bear heavily on sentencing under habitual criminal statutes. As noted above, requirements that the defendant have served a previous prison sentence could limit such terms to offenders whose previous offenses were serious or violent, since it may be assumed that general sentencing policies favor probation or suspended sentences for first offenders or for minor felonies. When one takes into account the wide disparities of sentencing that are common in U.S. courts, however, the conclusion must be that such requirements in fact decrease the consistency of application of habitual criminal statutes. A particular defendant may be subject to the statute not because his previous offenses were serious, but rather because he was sentenced in a court where prison sentences are common for relatively minor offenses.

Given the nature and extent of discretion involved in invoking and applying habitual criminal laws, along with the broad categories of offenses covered, the kind of discrimination against the poor or disadvantaged and against racial and ethnic minorities that has characterized the U.S. criminal justice systems in general may be expected to operate to a similar degree.[7]

Operating together, these factors lead to one conclusion: habitual criminal laws, since they do not even by their own terms attempt to distinguish violent from nonviolent offenders, and since they are subject to so much discretion, must be considered of little use in singling out and dealing with violent offenders.

Constitutional Issues

Habitual criminal acts have withstood numerous constitutional attacks over the years. These challenges have usually revolved around the issues of double jeopardy, equal protection, and cruel and unusual punishment. Double jeopardy challenges have been rejected repeatedly on the ground that recidivists "are not punished the second time for the earlier offense, but the repetition of criminal conduct aggravates their guilt and justifies heavier penalties when they are again convicted."[8]

Under the general rules of analysis applied to equal protection questions, treating recidivists differently from other classes of criminals has been held permissible as reasonably related to the legitimate purpose of protecting the public.[9] Katkin suggested that because of changes in constitutional theory and accumulating evidence that such statutes do not really provide the protection sought, reconsidering equal protection rationales might result in a reversal of this rule.[10]

No court has yet held a habitual criminal law to constitute cruel and unusual punishment on its face. A few, however, have found their application in specific cases to be cruel and usual. *Hart* v. *Coiner*, 483 F.2d 136 (4th Cir. 1973), involved a defendant sentenced to life imprisonment for his third felony, as required by the West Virginia statute in effect at the time. The defendant's three convictions were for writing an insufficient fund check for $50 in 1949, interstate transportation of forged checks worth $140 in 1955, and committing perjury in his son's murder trial in 1968.

The court found the statute constitutional on its face, noting that the same statute had been upheld on due process and equal protection challenges in previous cases. But the court ruled that imposing a life sentence on this defendant under the statute was "constitutionally excessive and wholly disproportionate to the nature of the offenses committed, and not necessary to achieve any legitimate legislative purpose."[11]

In reaching this result, the court discussed the proportionality aspects of cruel and unusual punishment decisions as outlined in *Weems* v. *U.S.*, 217 U.S. 349 (1910), and *Furman* v. *Georgia*, 408 U.S. 238 (1971). This test requires considering the punishment in light of the nature of the offense and also in comparison with punishments for other crimes of similar or greater seriousness. "In assessing the nature and gravity of an offense," said the *Hart* opinion, "courts have repeatedly emphasized the element of violence and danger to the person."[12] The court noted that "'there are rational gradations of culpability that can be made on the basis of injury to the victim.' None of Hart's offenses were against the person. None involved violence or danger of violence toward persons or property. The bad check case was very nearly trivial—one penny less in the face amount of the check and the offense would have been a five- to sixty-day petty misdemeanor."[13] The court rejected the state's argument that a punishment that serves a legitimate purpose—in this case, deterrence—cannot be cruel and unusual, noting that such an argument could be used to justify the harshest penalties for the most trivial offenses. "Life imprisonment is the penultimate punishment. Tradition, custom, and common sense reserve it for those violent persons who are dangerous to others. It is not a practical solution to petty crime in America. Aside from the proportionality principle, there aren't enough prisons in America to hold all the Harts that afflict us."[14]

The court quoted Justice William J. Brennan's opinion in *Furman* v. *Georgia*, 408 U.S. 238 (1971): "If there is a significantly less severe punishment to achieve the purposes for which the punishment is inflicted, the punishment inflicted is unnecessary and therefore excessive."[15] The *Hart* opinion then went on to say, "We think that a sentence of life imprisonment, the most severe punishment available under West Virginia law, is unnecessary to accomplish the legislative purpose to protect society from an individual who has committed three wholly nonviolent crimes over a period of twenty years. Nor, except on the theory that more is better, is it necessary to deter others."[16]

A dissenting opinion in *Hart* pointed out that the court on the same day had upheld two concurrent five-year-sentences for two counts of making obscene phone calls. In so doing, the court noted that the sentence might have been more severe because of the defendant's previous convictions of larceny and car theft, but it found the punishment not disproportionate and not cruel and unusual. The dissenter pointed out that the majority suggests no standards for what would be proportionate to Hart's offenses.

The *Hart* opinion may indicate that in the future courts will look more closely at sentences imposed under habitual criminal statutes, and may find more of them prohibited by the Eighth Amendment.

The opinion makes clear, however, that the court's objection is to applying the statute to nonviolent offenses. A habitual criminal statute imposing very long sentences on persons who have repeatedly committed violent crimes probably would encounter no serious constitutional problems. In fact, if courts were to follow the *Hart* rationale in the future, habitual criminal laws might become more effective in singling out violent offenders for special handling, either for rehabilitation or for incapacitation.

General Characteristics of the Model Penal Code Type

The second kind of recidivist statute is the Model Penal Code type, which takes a basically different approach to the problem. Five such statutes are in effect: the federal statute, and those of Hawaii, New Hampshire, North Dakota, and Oregon.[17] The proposals of Sec. 7.03 of the Model Penal Code (American Law Institute, Proposed Official Draft, 1962) and Sec. 5 of the Model Sentencing Act (National Council on Crime and Delinquency, 2nd. ed., 1972) will also be considered here.

These statutes differ from traditional statutes in a number of substantive and procedural respects. They require a special court decision on whether the added sentence is to be imposed; this decision is based on both retrospective factors involving previous criminal record and prospective factors involving the defendant's mental state and a prediction of future criminal behavior or use of violence. Most of the schemes require a psychiatric examination, and most also require formal notice to the defendant of the extended sentence sought by the state and of the type of evidence that will be presented to justify it. The statutes thus incorporate elements of traditional habitual criminal statutes, general sentencing authority of trial courts, and medical and predictive judgments typical of sexual psychopath statutes (discussed in chapter 2).

Model Penal Code

The Model Penal Code[18] provides for an extended term if the defendant falls into any of the following four categories:

1. The defendant is "a persistent offender whose commitment for an extended term is necessary for protection of the public." Such a finding requires a record of two previous felony convictions or one felony and two misdemeanors.
2. The defendant is "a professional criminal whose commitment for an extended term is necessary for protection of the public." This element may be proved by circumstances of the present offense showing "that the defendant has knowingly devoted himself to criminal activity as a major source of livelihood," or by substantial income or resources not shown to be derived from legal sources.
3. The defendant is "a dangerous, mentally abnormal person whose commitment for an extended term is necessary for protection of the public." Sentencing under this condition requires a psychiatric examination leading to the conclusion that the defendant is a serious danger to others because his mental condition is "gravely abnormal," and that his criminal conduct has been characterized by repetitive or compulsive behavior or by "persistent aggressive behavior with heedless indifference to the consequences."
4. The present charges involve multiple offenses or "extensive" criminality. This category requires that the defendant be presently subject to two or more sentences that will run concurrently, or that maximum sentences for the present offenses, if served consecutively, would exceed the extended term imposed, or that the defendant admit in open court other felonies that he wishes to be taken into account in sentencing. [Although it is difficult to understand why a defendant would ever make such an admission, Sec. 7.03 (4)(b) refers to it.]

The first of these categories is similar to traditional habitual criminal statutes; the third is similar to the grounds for civil-type commitments to mental institutions under sexual psychopath statutes. The fourth does not go much farther than the general authority of courts to order that sentences be served consecutively. The second involves elements that are frequently considered in sentencing decisions but would not justify imposing a sentence longer than the maximum for the present offense.

Federal Criminal Code

The federal statute requires that the defendant be found to be both a "special offender" and a "dangerous offender" before the longer sentence may be imposed.[19]

Any of the following three circumstances is sufficient to make the defendant a "special offender":

1. The defendant has two previous convictions for offenses punishable by death or imprisonment for more than one year, and was imprisoned for at least one of these offenses, and the present offense was committed within five years of a previous offense or within five years of his release from imprisonment for a previous offense.
2. The present offense was part of a pattern of criminal conduct "which constituted a substantial source of his income, and in which he manifested special skill or expertise."
3. The present felony involved a conspiracy with three or more other persons, and the defendant did, or agreed to do, one of the following: "initiate, organize, plan, finance, direct, manage, or supervise all or part of such conspiracy or conduct, or give or receive a bribe or use force as all or part of such conduct."

A defendant is defined to be a "dangerous offender" if "a period of confinement longer than that provided for such felony is required for the protection of the public from further criminal conduct by the defendant."

The statute includes detailed standards for determining when a defendant has a substantial source of income from criminal activities, what constitutes special skill or expertise in criminal activity, and what a pattern of criminal conduct is. In addition, the statute provides specific requirements for advance notice to the defendant of the request for imposition of the extended sentence; presentation of information in support of it; the defendant's rights to counsel, compulsory process and cross-examination of hearing witnesses; the circumstances under which part or all of a presentence report may be withheld from the defendant; inclusion in the record of the court's findings and reasons for imposing the sentence selected; and procedure for obtaining review of sentences.

The court is authorized to impose the extended sentence "if it appears by a preponderance of the information, including information submitted during the trial . . . and the sentencing hearing and so much of the presentence report as the court relies upon, that the defendant is a dangerous special offender. . . ."

Section 3577 reads as follows: "No limitation shall be placed on the information concerning the background, character, and conduct of a person convicted of an offense which a court of the United States may receive and consider for the purpose of imposing an appropriate sentence."

The North Dakota Statute

The North Dakota statute reveals substantial borrowing from the Model Penal Code and the federal statute.[20] Its categories of "dangerous special offenders" include the Model Penal Code groups of "persistent offenders," "dangerous, mentally abnormal persons," and "professional criminals," and also two others:

1. Defendants whose present offense "seriously endangered the life of another person" and who have previously been convicted of similar offenses.
2. Defendants who are "especially dangerous" because they used a firearm, dangerous weapon, or destructive device in the commission of the offense or in flight following the offense.

Any one of these circumstances is sufficient to authorize the imposition of the extended sentence.

The language of the North Dakota statute setting out the required procedure is identical to that in the federal statute, although some of the items appear in different order. Except for a few minor changes, the Hawaii statute is identical to the Model Penal Code. The New Hampshire and Oregon statutes and the Model Sentencing Act involve the same elements, in differing combinations.

Penalties

The authorized sentences of the Model Penal Code type statutes are as follows:

Model Penal Code—length not specified.

Model Sentencing Act—up to thirty years.

Federal statute—up to twenty-five years "and not disproportionate in severity to the maximum term otherwise authorized" for the present offense.

Hawaii statute—a life term for a Class A felony; twenty years for a Class B felony, and ten years for a Class C felony.

New Hampshire statute—a life term for murder; ten to thirty years for a felony; two to five years for a misdemeanor.

North Dakota statute—up to life for a Class A felony; up to twenty years for a Class B felony, and up to ten years for a Class C felony.

Oregon statute—thirty years.

Usefulness

The elaborate procedure that must be followed before a defendant may be sentenced under Model Penal Code-type statutes probably means that such statutes are not likely to be used against offenders whose crimes are not serious (although the New Hampshire statute does provide penalties for misdemeanors). However, the inclusion of classes of professional criminals and persistent offenders, as well as violent offenders, demonstrates that the statutes were intended for use against persons whose continuing criminality may pose no direct threat to others' lives or personal safety. The federal statute is part of the Organized Crime Control Act of 1970, and clearly it was intended for use against offenders who had not committed crimes of violence. Note that the language of 18 U.S.C. 3575 (f) defining "dangerous offender" speaks of protecting the public from "further criminal conduct by the defendant," not from further violent conduct. Several factors involved in "special skill or expertise in criminal conduct" are not necessarily related to offenses against the person.

Constitutional and Ethical Issues

Constitutional questions concerning such statutes have been raised in cases under the federal statute. A federal district court declared the statute unconstitutional in *U.S.* v. *Duardi*, 384 F. Supp. 874, (W.D. Mo. 1974).[21] The court found the following infirmities in the statute: the possibility of imposing punishment, through a finding of dangerousness for allegedly criminal activities (1) in violation of the Sixth Amendment right to a speedy, public trial by an impartial jury, (2) without the fundamental due process protection of the reasonable doubt standard, (3) in derogation of a due process right not to be tried on the basis of information unrestricted by the rules of evidence, and (4) pursuant to a standard established by Sec. 3575 (f), which is so unduly vague and uncertain that it violates due process.[22]

The court's most serious concern was the kind of information the government offered as a basis for imposing the extended sentence. It characterized this information as "the testimony of F.B.I. and Bureau of Narcotics Agents as to what faceless informants told them about alleged contacts with particular defendants" and "certain alleged criminal conduct of the defendants" for which they had been neither tried nor convicted.[23] The court stated its ruling as follows: "[W]e find . . . that it would be constitutionally impermissible for this Court, sitting without a jury, to make a finding of 'dangerousness' under § 3575 (f) based upon 'information' that defendants may, if charged and tried, be found guilty of the crimes alleged in the government's amended notice."[24] As of this writing, *Duardi* is on appeal to the Eighth Circuit.[25]

The federal sentencing procedure has been upheld by the Sixth Circuit, which held that the term "dangerous" as used in the statute is not unconstitutionally vague.[26] The U.S. District Court for Northern Texas has also upheld the statute, ruling that the term "dangerous" is neither unduly vague nor overbroad, and that the "preponderance of the information" standard is appropriate for information considered in sentencing decisions.[27]

At issue in all these cases is the nature of the procedure established by Sec. 3575. If the proceeding is a sentencing decision in the usual sense, the kinds of due process rights enumerated above would not apply.[28] If Sec. 3575 creates a new and separate charge, however, the defendant would be entitled to all the protections of a criminal trial in the decision whether he is a "special dangerous offender" subject to the enhanced sentence.

Some of the constitutional issues now being litigated pose ethical questions as well. For example, the federal statute proposes to use information concerning other criminal activity in addition to the instant offense as a basis for imposing the longer sentence. If such information is not the type that would support additional criminal charges leading to prison sentences, by what justification can it be used to impose a prison sentence without such criminal charges? The statute seems to be an attempt to transform insufficient evidence for conviction and imprisonment into sufficient evidence for imprisonment without conviction.

Further, any scheme for confining an offender because of some prediction of future criminal activity, based either on psychiatric evidence or on criminal record, runs afoul of all the problems of overprediction and preventive detention.[29] If such decisions are to be made, and persons are to be deprived of their liberty on this kind of evidence, surely one can argue that the decisions ought to be made much more consciously and openly than is contemplated in statutes that purport to deal only with sentencing for specific offenses.

Notes

1. *House of Commons, Report of the Committee on Prisons, 1895.*

2. Daniel Katkin, "Habitual Offender Laws: A Reconsideration," 21 *Buffalo Law Review* 99 (1971).

3. 1926 N.Y. Session Laws, Ch. 457, see "The Treatment of the Recidivist in the United States," 23 *Canadian Bar Review* 640, 642 (1945).

4. Code Ala., Tit. 15, § 331; Alas. Stat. 12.55.040; Ark. Stat. Ann. 43-2328; Ariz. Rev. Stat. 13-1649; Cal. Pen. Code 644; Colo. Rev. Stat. 16-13-101; Conn. Gen. Stat. Ann. 53a-40; Del. Code Ann. Tit. 11, §§ 4214, 4215; Fla. Stat. Ann. 775.09; Ga. Code Ann. 27-2511; Idaho Code 19-2514; Ind. Code 35-8-8-1; Iowa Code Ann. 747.1; Kan. Stat. Ann. 21-4504; Ky. Rev. Stat. Ann. 532.080; West's La. Stat. Ann. 15:529.1; Me. Rev. Stat. Ann. Tit. 15, § 1742; Mich. Comp. Laws Ann. 769.10; Minn. Stat. Ann. 609.155, 609.16; Vernon's Ann. Mo. Stat. 556.280; Rev. Codes Mont. Ann. 95-1507; Rev. Stat. Neb. 29-221; N.J. Stat. Ann. 2A:85-12, 2A:85-13; N.M. Stat. Ann. 40A-29-5; McKinney's N.Y. Pen. Code Ann. 70.10; Nev. Rev. Stat. 207.010; Gen. Stat. N.C. 14-7.1 to 14-7.6; Okla. Stat. Ann. Chap. 21.§ 51; Gen. Laws R.I. 12-19-21; Code Laws S.C. 17-553.1; S.D. Comp. Laws 22-7-1 to 22-7-5; Tenn. Code Ann. 40-2801 et seq.; Vernon's Tex. Pen. Code Ann. 12.42; Vt. Stat. Ann. Tit. 13 § 11; Rev. Code Wash. Ann. 9.92.090; W. Va. Code 61-11-18; Wis. Stat. Ann. 939.62; Wyo. Stat. 6-9; 22 D.C. Code 104, 104a; Laws P.R. Ann. Tit. 33§ 131.

5. Katkin, "Habitual Offender Laws," pp. 106-109.

6. Ibid., p. 109.

7. See *Furman* v. *Georgia*, 408 U.S. 238 (1971), concurring opinion of Justice Douglas, pp. 249-257.

8. *Graham* v. *West Virginia*, 224 U.S. 616, 623 (1912).

9. *State* v. *Sandoval*, 80 N.M. 333, 455 P. 2d 837 (1969).

10. Katkin, "Habitual Offender Laws," p. 111.

11. 483 F.2d at 143.

12. 483 F.2d at 140.

13. 483 F.2d at 141.

14. 483 F.2d at 141.

15. 483 F.2d at 141.

16. 483 F.2d at 141.

17. 18 U.S.C. 3575, Hawaii 1972 Session Laws, Act 9, Sec. 662, p. 80; N.H. Rev. Stat. Ann. 651:6; N.D. Century Code 12. 1-32-09, Ore. Rev. Stat. 161.725, 166.735.

18. See Appendix 1B.

19. See Appendix 1A.

20. See Appendix 1D.

21. See also 384 F. Supp. 856 (W.D. Mo 1973), 384 F. Supp. 86 (W.D. Mo. 1973), 384 F. Supp. 871 (W.D. Mo. 1974).

22. "Constitutional Problems in Enhanced Sentencing for 'Dangerous Special Offenders,'" 40 *Missouri Law Review* 660 (1975).

23. 384 F. Supp. at 881.

24. 384 F. Supp at 883.

25. No. 75-1354.

26. *U.S.* v. *Stewart*, 531 F.2d 326 (D.C. Cir. 1976).

27. *U.S.* v. *Holt*, 397 F. Supp. 1397 (N.D. Tex., 1975).

28. See *Williams* v. *New York*, 337 U.S. 241 (1949).

29. See Andrew Von Hirsch, "Prediction of Criminal Conduct and Preventive Confinement of Convicted Persons," 21 *Buffalo Law Review* 717 (1972); Alan Dershowitz, "Preventive Confinement: A Suggested Framework for Constitutional Analysis," 51 *Texas Law Review* 1277 (1973).

Appendix 1A:
18 U.S.C. 3575, Increased Sentence for Dangerous Special Offenders

(a) Whenever an attorney charged with the prosecution of a defendant in a court of the United States for an alleged felony committed when the defendant was over the age of twenty-one years has reason to believe that the defendant is a dangerous special offender such attorney, a reasonable time before trial or acceptance by the court of a plea of guilty or nolo contendere, may sign and file with the court, and may amend, a notice (1) specifying that the defendant is a dangerous special offender who upon conviction for such felony is subject to the imposition of a sentence under subsection (b) of this section, and (2) setting out with particularity the reasons why such attorney believes the defendant to be a dangerous special offender. In no case shall the fact that the defendant is alleged to be a dangerous special offender be an issue upon the trial of such felony, be disclosed to the jury, or be disclosed before any plea of guilty or nolo contendere or verdict or finding of guilty to the presiding judge without the consent of the parties. If the court finds that the filing of the notice as a public record may prejudice fair consideration of a pending criminal matter, it may order the notice sealed and the notice shall not be subject to subpena or public inspection during the pendency of such criminal matter, except on order of the court, but shall be subject to inspection by the defendant alleged to be a dangerous special offender and his counsel.

(b) Upon any plea of guilty or nolo contendere or verdict or finding of guilty of the defendant of such felony, a hearing shall be held, before sentence is imposed, by the court sitting without a jury. The court shall fix a time for the hearing, and notice thereof shall be given to the defendant and the United States at least ten days prior thereto. The court shall permit the United States and counsel for the defendant, or the defendant if he is not represented by counsel, to inspect the presentence report sufficiently prior to the hearing as to afford a reasonable opportunity for verification. In extraordinary cases, the court may withhold material not relevant to a proper sentence, diagnostic opinion which might seriously disrupt a program of rehabilitation, any source of information obtained on a promise of confidentiality, and material previously disclosed in open court. A court withholding all or part of a presentence report shall inform the parties of its action and place in the record the reasons therefor. The court may require parties inspecting all or part of a presentence report to give notice of any part thereof intended to be controverted. In connection with the hearing, the defendant and the United States shall be entitled to assistance of counsel, compulsory process, and cross-examination of such witnesses as appear at the hearing. A duly authenticated copy of a former judgment or commitment shall be prima facie evidence of such former judgment or commitment. If it appears by a preponderance of the information, including information submitted during the trial of such felony and the sentencing hearing and so much of the presentence report as the court relies upon, that the defendant is a dangerous special offender, the court shall sentence the defendant to imprisonment for an appropriate term not to exceed twenty-five years and not disproportionate in severity to the maximum term otherwise authorized by law for such felony. Otherwise it shall sentence the defendant in accordance with the law prescribing penalties for such felony. The court shall place in the record its findings, including an identification of the information relied upon in making such findings, and its reasons for the sentence imposed.

(c) This section shall not prevent the imposition and execution of a sentence of death or of imprisonment for life or for a term exceeding twenty-five years upon any person convicted of an offense so punishable.

(d) Notwithstanding any other provision of this section, the court shall not sentence a dangerous special offender to less than any mandatory penalty prescribed by law for such felony. This section shall not be construed as creating any mandatory minimum penalty.

(e) A defendant is a special offender for purposes of this section if—
   (1) the defendant has previously been convicted in courts of the United States, a State, the District of Columbia, the Commonwealth of Puerto Rico, a territory or possession of the United States, any political subdivision, or any department, agency, or instrumentality thereof for two or more offenses committed on occasions different from one another and from such felony and punishable in such courts by death or imprisonment in excess of one year, for one or more of such convictions the defendant has been imprisoned prior to the commission of such felony, and less than five years have elapsed between the commission of such felony and either the defendant's release, on parole or otherwise, from imprisonment for one such conviction or his commission of the last such previous offense or another offense punishable by death or imprisonment in excess of one year under applicable laws of the United States, a State, the District of Columbia, the Commonwealth of Puerto Rico, a territory or possession of the United States, any political subdivision, or any department, agency or instrumentality thereof; or
   (2) the defendant committed such felony as part of a pattern of conduct which was criminal under applicable laws of any jurisdiction, which constituted a substantial source of his income, and in which he manifested special skill or expertise; or
   (3) such felony was, or the defendant committed such felony in furtherance

of, a conspiracy with three or more other persons to engage in a pattern of conduct criminal under applicable laws of any jurisdiction, and the defendant did, or agreed that he would, initiate, organize, plan, finance, direct, manage, or supervise all or part of such conspiracy or conduct, or give or receive a bribe or use force as all or part of such conduct.

A conviction shown on direct or collateral review or at the hearing to be invalid or for which the defendant has been pardoned on the ground of innocence shall be disregarded for purposes of paragraph (1) of this subsection. In support of findings under paragraph (2) of this subsection, it may be shown that the defendant has had in his own name or under his control income or property not explained as derived from a source other than such conduct. For purposes of paragraph (2) of this subsection, a substantial source of income means a source of income which for any period of one year or more exceeds the minimum wage, determined on the basis of a forty-hour week and a fifty-week year, without reference to exceptions, under section 6(a) (1) of the Fair Labor Standards Act of 1938 (52 Stat. 1602, as amended 80 Stat. 838), and as hereafter amended, for an employee engaged in commerce or in the production of goods for commerce, and which for the same period exceeds fifty percent of the defendant's declared adjusted gross income under section 62 of the Internal Revenue Act of 1954 (68A Stat. 17, as amended 83 Stat. 655), and as hereafter amended. For purposes of paragraph (2) of this subsection, special skill or expertise in criminal conduct includes unusual knowledge, judgment or ability, including manual dexterity, facilitating the initiation, organizing, planning, financing, direction, management, supervision, execution or concealment of criminal conduct, the enlistment of accomplices in such conduct, the escape from detection or apprehension for such conduct, or the disposition of the fruits or proceeds of such conduct. For purposes of paragraphs (2) and (3) of this subsection, criminal conduct forms a pattern if it embraces criminal acts that have the same or similar purposes, results, participants, victims, or methods of commission, or otherwise are interrelated by distinguishing characteristics and are not isolated events.

(f) A defendant is dangerous for purposes of this section if a period of confinement longer than that provided for such felony is required for the protection of the public from further criminal conduct by the defendant.

(g) The time for taking an appeal from a conviction for which sentence is imposed after proceedings under this section shall be measured from imposition of the original sentence.

3576. Review of Sentence

With respect to the imposition, correction, or reduction of a sentence after proceedings under section 3575 of this chapter, a review of the sentence on the record of the sentencing court may be taken by the defendant or the United States to a court of appeals. Any review of the sentence taken by the United States shall be taken at least five days before expiration of the time for taking a review of the sentence or appeal of the conviction by the defendant and shall be diligently prosecuted. The sentencing court may, with or without motion and notice, extend the time for taking a review of the sentence for a period not to exceed thirty days from the expiration of the time otherwise prescribed by law. The court shall not extend the time for taking a review of the sentence by the United States after the time has expired. A court extending the time for taking a review of the sentence by the United States shall extend the time for taking a review of the sentence or appeal of the conviction by the defendant for the same period. The taking of a review of the sentence by the United States shall be deemed the taking of a review of the sentence and an appeal of the conviction by the defendant. Review of the sentence shall include review of whether the procedure employed was lawful, the findings made were clearly erroneous, or the sentencing court's discretion was abused. The court of appeals on review of the sentence may, after considering the record, including the entire presentence report, information submitted during the trial of such felony and the sentencing hearing, and the findings and reasons of the sentencing court, affirm the sentence, impose or direct the imposition of any sentence which the sentencing court could originally have imposed, or remand for further sentencing proceedings and imposition of sentence, except that a sentence may be made more severe only on review of the sentence taken by the United States and after hearing. Failure of the United States to take a review of the imposition of the sentence shall, upon review taken by the United States of the correction or reduction of the sentence, foreclose imposition of a sentence more severe than that reviewed but shall not otherwise foreclose the review of the sentence or the appeal of the conviction. The court of appeals shall state in writing the reasons for its disposition of the review of the sentence. Any review of the sentence taken by the United States may be dismissed on a showing of abuse of the right of the United States to take such review.

3577. Use of Information for Sentencing

No limitation shall be placed on the information concerning the background, character, and conduct of a person convicted of an offense which a court of the United States may receive and consider for the purpose of imposing an appropriate sentence.

[Sec. 3578, concerning maintenance of records of convictions, is omitted.]

Appendix 1B:
Model Penal Code, Sec. 7.03,
Criteria for Sentence of
Extended Term of
Imprisonment; Felonies

The Court may sentence a person who has been convicted of a felony to an extended term of imprisonment if it finds one or more of the grounds specified in this section. The finding of the Court shall be incorporated in the record.

(1) The defendant is a persistent offender whose commitment for an extended term is necessary for protection of the public.

The Court shall not make such a finding unless the defendant is over twenty-one years of age and has previously been convicted of two felonies or of one felony and two misdemeanors, committed at different times when he was over [insert Juvenile Court age] years of age.

(2) The defendant is a professional criminal whose commitment for an extended term is necessary for protection of the public.

The Court shall not make such a finding unless the defendant is over twenty-one years of age and:

(a) the circumstances of the crime show that the defendant has knowingly devoted himself to criminal activity as a major source of livelihood; or

(b) the defendant has substantial income or resources not explained to be derived from a source other than criminal activity.

(3) The defendant is a dangerous, mentally abnormal person whose commitment for an extended term is necessary for protection of the public.

The Court shall not make such a finding unless the defendant has been subjected to a psychiatric examination resulting in the conclusions that his mental condition is gravely abnormal; that his criminal conduct has been characterized by a pattern of repetitive or compulsive behavior or by persistent aggressive behavior with heedless indifference to consequences; and that such condition makes him a serious danger to others.

(4) The defendant is a multiple offender whose criminality was so extensive that a sentence of imprisonment for an extended term is warranted.

The Court shall not make such a finding unless:

(a) the defendant is being sentenced for two or more felonies, or is already under sentence of imprisonment for felony, and the sentences of imprisonment involved will run concurrently under Section 7.06; or

(b) the defendant admits in open court the commission of one or more other felonies and asks that they be taken into account when he is sentenced; and

(c) the longest sentences of imprisonment authorized for each of the defendant's crimes, including admitted crimes taken into account, if made to run consecutively would exceed in length the minimum and maximum of the extended term imposed.

Appendix 1C: Model Sentencing Act, Sec. 5, Dangerous Offenders

Except for the crime of murder in the first degree, the court may sentence a defendant to a term of commitment of years stated but not more than thirty years if either of the following grounds is found to exist:

(1) The defendant is being sentenced for a felony in which he

(a) inflicted or attempted to inflict serious bodily harm or

(b) seriously endangered the life or safety of another and he was previously convicted of one or more felonies not related to the instant crime as a single criminal episode, and

(c) the court finds that he is suffering from a severe mental or emotional disorder indicating a propensity toward continuing dangerous criminal activity.

Whenever the court, upon entering the conviction or receiving the investigation report, has reason to believe the defendant falls within the category of subdivision 1 (a) or 1 (b), it shall refer him to [diagnostic facility] for study and report as to whether he is suffering from a severe mental or emotional disorder indicating a propensity toward continuing dangerous criminal activity. Such referral shall not exceed ninety days, subject to additional extensions not exceeding ninety days on order of the court. The defendant shall not be sentenced under subdivision 1 (a) or 1 (b) unless the judge, after considering the presentence investigation, the report of the diagnostic center, and the evidence in the case and at the sentencing hearing, finds that the defendant comes within the purview of subdivision 1 (a) or 1 (b) and 1 (c) and is therefore in need of correctional treatment or custody for a prolonged period. The findings shall be incorporated in the record.

(2) The defendant is being sentenced for a felony committed as part of a continuing criminal activity in concert with five or more persons, the defendant having been in a management or supervision position or having given legal, accounting, or other managerial counsel or, as a public servant, having unlawfully done or omitted to do anything in order to promote the criminal activity.

No sentence shall be imposed under this section unless the prosecuting attorney has notified the defendant in writing, in advance of the trial or a plea of guilty, that the prosecution intends to ask for an extended sentence under this section in the event of the defendant's conviction.

Any commitment shall be to the custody of [director of correction].

Appendix 1D:
North Dakota Century Code, Sec. 12.1-32-09, Dangerous Special Offenders—Extended Sentences—Procedure

1.   A court may sentence a convicted offender to an extended sentence as a dangerous special offender in accordance with the provisions of this section upon a finding of any one or more of the following:

a. The convicted offender is a dangerous, mentally abnormal person. The court shall not make such a finding unless the presentence report, including a psychiatric examination, concludes that the offender's conduct has been characterized by persistent aggressive behavior, and that such behavior makes him a serious danger to other persons.

b. The convicted offender is a professional criminal. The court shall not make such a finding unless the offender is an adult and the presentence report shows that the offender has substantial income or resources derived from criminal activity.

c. The convicted offender is a persistent offender. The court shall not make such a finding unless the offender is an adult and has previously been convicted in any state or states or by the United States of two felonies of class B or above, or of one class B felony or above plus two offenses potentially punishable by imprisonment classified below class B felony, committed at different times when the offender was an adult. For the purposes of this subdivision, a felony conviction in another state or under the laws of the United States shall be considered a felony of class B or above if it is punishable by a maximum term of imprisonment of ten years or more.

d. The offender was convicted of an offense which seriously endangered the life of another person, and the offender had previously been convicted of a similar offense.

e. The offender is especially dangerous because he used a firearm, dangerous weapon, or destructive device in the commission of the offense or during the flight therefrom.

A conviction shown on direct or collateral review or at the hearing to be invalid or for which the offender has been pardoned on the ground of innocence shall be disregarded for purposes of subdivision c. In support of findings under subdivision b, it may be shown that the offender has had in his own name or under his control income or property not explained as derived from a source other than criminal activity. For purposes of subdivision b, a substantial source of income means a source of income which for any period of one year or more exceeds the minimum wage, determined on the basis of a forty-hour week and a fifty-week year, without reference to exceptions, under section 7 (a) (1) of the Fair Labor Standards Act of 1938 as amended, for an employee engaged in commerce or in the production of goods for commerce, and which for the same period exceeds fifty percent of the offender's declared adjusted gross income under chapter 57-38.

2.   The extended sentence may be imposed in the following manner:

a. If the offense for which the offender is convicted is a class A felony, the court may impose a sentence up to a maximum of life imprisonment.

b. If the offense for which the offender is convicted is a class B felony, the court may impose a sentence up to a maximum of imprisonment for twenty years.

c. If the offense for which the offender is convicted is a class C felony, the court may impose a sentence up to a maximum of imprisonment for ten years.

3.   Whenever an attorney charged with the prosecution of a defendant in a court of this state for an alleged felony committed when the defendant was over the age of eighteen years has reason to believe that the defendant is a dangerous special offender, such attorney, at a reasonable time before trial or acceptance by the court of a plea of guilty, may sign and file with the court, and may amend, a notice specifying that the defendant is a dangerous special offender who upon conviction for such felony is subject to the imposition of a sentence under subsection 2, and setting out with particularity the reasons why such attorney believes the defendant to be a dangerous special offender. In no case shall the fact that the prosecuting attorney is seeking sentencing of the defendant as a dangerous special offender be disclosed to the jury, or be disclosed, before any plea of guilty or verdict or finding of guilt, to the presiding judge without the consent of the parties. If the court finds that the filing of the notice as a public record may prejudice fair consideration of a pending criminal matter, it may order the notice sealed and the notice shall not be subject to subpoena or public inspection during the pendency of such criminal matter, except on order of the court, but shall be subject to inspection by the defendant alleged to be a dangerous special offender and his counsel.

4.   Upon any plea of guilty, or verdict or finding of guilt of the defendant of such felony, a hearing shall be held, before sentence is imposed, by the court sitting without a jury. Except in the most extraordinary cases, the court shall obtain a presentence report and may receive a diagnostic testing report under subsection 4 of section 12.1-32-02 before holding a hearing under this subsection. The court shall fix a time for the hearing, and notice thereof shall be given to the defendant and the prosecution at least five days prior thereto. The court shall permit the prosecution and counsel for the defendant, or the defendant if he is not represented by counsel, to inspect the presentence report sufficiently prior to the hearing as to afford a reasonable opportunity for verification. In extraordinary cases, the court may withhold material not relevant to a proper sentence, diagnostic opinion which seriously disrupt a program of rehabilitation, any source of information obtained on a promise of confidentiality, and material previously disclosed in open court. A court withholding all or part of a presentence report shall inform the parties of its action and place in the record the reasons therefor. The court may require parties inspecting all or part of a presentence report to give notice of any part thereof intended to be controverted. In connection with the hearing, the defendant shall be entitled to compulsory process, and cross-examination of such witnesses as appear at the hearing. A duly authenticated copy of a former judgment or commitment shall be prima facie evidence of such former judgment or commitment. If it appears by a preponderance of the information, including information submitted during the trial of such felony and the sentencing hearing and so much of the presentence report as the court relies upon, that the defendant is a dangerous special offender, the court shall sentence the defendant to imprisonment for an appropriate term within the limits specified in subsection 2. The court shall place in the record its findings including an identification of the information relied upon in making such findings, and its reasons for the sentence imposed.

2 Sexual Psychopath Statutes

Introduction

Sexual psychopath statutes are important to this study because they represent a concerted attempt to deal with a special class of offenders thought to be especially dangerous. The drafters of the statutes attempted to designate a class of offenders thought to pose a special threat and to use progressive, scientific means to isolate them from the public and to cure them of the qualities that made them dangerous. Even though critics have maintained that the statutes did not and do not accomplish their purposes, it is essential to consider them in any study of the control of violent offenders.

This study classifies as sexual psychopath statutes those statutory schemes that meet all or most of the following requirements:

1. They are based on a definition ("sexual psychopath," "psychopathic offender," "mentally disordered sex offender," "criminal sexual deviant," or the like) involving mental abnormality or deficiency, coupled with propensities for the commission of sex offenses or other offenses, and often including mention of danger to other persons.
2. They provide for commitment, often indeterminate, to a mental hospital or special treatment facility.
3. They rely more on a psychiatric diagnosis of the subject's mental status than on usual criminal fact-finding procedures focusing on the act that constituted the crime.
4. The stated emphasis of the confinement is therapeutic rather than punitive, and release is conditioned more on improvement in the subject's condition or a decrease in his dangerousness as assessed by medical or psychological staff than on expiration of a period of time specified by the court.

Many sexual psychopath statutes are limited to offenders who have committed sex offenses or who are thought to be dangerous only in the sense of a threat of molestation of children or sexual assault. They adopt the medical model of dealing with offenders, and they rely for their legal justification on the *parens patriae* doctrine. Although protecting the public from such offenders is clearly a major purpose of such laws, they are usually considered to have a benevolent rather than a retributive purpose, and to provide benefits to the offender sufficient to justify confining him and treating him against his will.

41

Most sexual psychopath statutes include a definition of the class of persons subject to commitment. In most states the statutes apply to persons charged with, or convicted of, any of a group of offenses specified in the statute. Procedure is outlined for suspension of the criminal prosecution, referral of the subject for psychiatric examination, submission of a medical report to the court, and a hearing to determine whether the subject falls within the class defined, and whether he should be committed. The statutes cover due process rights such as the right to counsel, the right to inspect reports and other documents, the right to an independent medical examination, and the right to appeal the commitment.

Additionally, the statutes usually specify the kind of institution to which the subject is committed, the frequency of required reports on his condition and progress, the rights he holds as a mental patient, and procedures for conditional release and final discharge from the institution. They also may provide for the disposition of criminal charges after final discharge.

The theory and purposes of sexual psychopath statutes are perhaps best described in *Director* v. *Daniels* 243 Md. 16, 221 A.2d 397, cert. den. 385 U.S. 940 (1966), a case arising under Maryland's Defective Delinquent Statute, probably the best known of all such statutes. The court says that it has long been recognized that there is a group of offenders who are legally sane and therefore responsible for their acts but who persist in antisocial behavior and who do not respond to traditional penal or reformative measures.

... [T]he statute rejects the age-old concept that every legally sane person possesses in equal degree the free will to choose between doing right and doing wrong. Instead, it substitutes the concept that there is a category of legally sane persons who by reason of mental or emotional deficiencies "evidence a propensity toward criminal activity," which they are incapable of controlling. For those in the category who are treatable it would substitute psychiatric treatment for punishment in the conventional sense and would free them from confinement not when they have "paid their debt to society," but when they have been sufficiently cured to make it reasonably safe to release them. With this humanitarian and progressive approach to the problem no person who has deplored the inadequacies of conventional penological practices can complain.[1]

In spite of this optimistic assessment, sexual psychopath laws have been the target of a continuing barrage of objections ever since the first few were enacted. These objections have been constitutional, ethical, and practical; to a great extent they reflect the disagreement between proponents of punitive or "justice" models of social control, with their emphasis on procedure and proportionality, and therapeutic or medical models. This chapter will cover the major factors in the constitutional and ethical debates, and at least suggest some of the other controversies.

Because of the number and complexity of constitutional issues with respect to sexual psychopath laws and the ways in which many of these issues are interrelated, we will attempt merely to suggest them in the description of the statutes, and to return to them in detail in the latter part of the chapter. Since persons who are committed, or whose commitment is sought, may or may not be defendants in criminal proceedings, all will be referred to here as subjects of the sexual psychopath proceedings. At present, there are twenty-seven sexual psychopath statutes in effect in twenty-six U.S. jurisdictions.[2] (Minnesota has two such statutes, the Psychopathic Personality Statute, § 526.09, and the Sex Offenders Act, § 246.43. The state of Washington, in addition to the act cited above, has a psychopathic delinquent statute for juveniles, § 71.06.150, which will not be discussed in this paper.)

Historical Background

Sexual psychopath-type statutes were enacted in two waves in the United States. The first wave began with the passage of the Briggs Act in Massachusetts in 1911,[3] which was followed by a similar statute in New York. These statutes were directed largely toward "mental defectives" and the "feeble-minded," and they placed less emphasis on sex offenses than present statutes do. Nicholas Kittrie says:

Originally the [New York] act provided for commitment either before or after conviction. But claims that feeble-minded persons were being committed on trumped-up charges for the purpose of relieving relatives and friends of support resulted in making prior conviction a prerequisite for confinement. The defective delinquent statutes usually make no distinctions between the types of crimes committed by the habitual offenders (whether sexual or nonsexual), but their applicability is restricted to those delinquents suffering from some intellectual deficiency.[4]

The second wave of statutes, those properly characterized as *sexual* psychopath statutes, came in the late 1930s. The first of these was passed in Michigan in 1937.[a] Within a few years, such laws had been passed in a number of other states.[b]

These statutes represent one aspect of the general trend away from the punitive approach in the control of social ills and toward a "benevolent" or therapeutic approach that has been apparent in this country during most of this century. They rely on a number of theories about the nature of sex offenders that have been advanced by members of the psychiatric and psychological fraternity, and also, in later years, vehemently attacked by others of the same group. Edwin Sutherland listed these assumptions as follows:

[a]After this statute was declared unconstitutional in 1938, in *People* v. *Frontczak*, 286 Mich. 51, 281 N.W. 534 (1938), a revised law was enacted in 1939; the second statute was upheld. *People* v. *Chapman*, 301 Mich. 584, 4 N.W. 2d 18 (1942).

[b]Illinois, 1938; California and Minnesota, 1939; Vermont, 1943; Ohio, 1945; Massachusetts, Washington, and Wisconsin, 1947; District of Columbia, 1948; Indiana, New Hampshire, and New Jersey, 1949.

1. Women and children are in great danger in American society because serious sex crimes are very prevalent and are increasing more rapidly than any other type of crime . . . .
2. Practically all of these serious sex crimes are committed by "degenerates," "sex fiends," or "sexual psychopaths . . . ."
3. These sexual psychopaths continue to commit serious sex crimes through life because they have no control over their sexual impulses; they have a mental malady and are not responsible for their behavior.
4. A sexual psychopath can be identified with a high degree of precision even before he has committed any sex crimes.
5. A society which punishes sex criminals, even with severe penalties, and then releases them to prey again upon women and children is failing in its duty.
6. Laws should be enacted to segregate such persons, preferably before but at least after their sex crimes, and to keep them confined as irresponsible patients until their malady has been completely and permanently cured.
7. Since sexual psychopathy is a mental malady, the professional advice as to the diagnosis, the treatment, and the release of patients as cured should come exclusively from psychiatrists.[5]

After enumerating these premises, Sutherland concluded: "All of these propositions, which are implicit in the laws and explicit in the popular literature, are either false or questionable."[6] These assumptions have been challenged from other quarters as well,[7] and a number of commentators have maintained that the concept of "psychopath" itself has no clearly ascertainable meaning. Some of these objections, and their implications for the legal status of sexual psychopath laws, will be considered in more detail later.

Sutherland described the factors that led to enactment of sexual psychopath laws in such a short period.[8] The statutes usually have their origins in a state of public fear following upon "a few serious sex crimes committed in quick succession."[9] Sutherland noted that this type of fear is almost never related to statistical trends in the total rate of sex crimes, but rather to the publicity that follows a few specific crimes, especially if the victims are children.

Sutherland went on to say that

The diffusion of sexual psychopath laws, consequently, has occurred under the following conditions: a state of fear developed, to some extent, by a general, nation-wide popular literature and made explicit by a few spectacular sex crimes; a series of scattered and conflicting reactions by many individuals and groups within the community; the appointment of a committee which in some cases has been guided by psychiatrists, which organizes existing information regarding sex crimes and the precedents for their control and which presents a sexual psychopath law to the legislature and to the public as the most scientific and enlightened method of protecting society against dangerous sex criminals. The organization of information in the name of science and without critical appraisal seems to be more invariably related to the emergence of a sexual psychopath law than is any other part of this genetic process.[10]

The information organized and presented is frequently the set of questionable assumptions listed above.

Sutherland listed psychitrists as the major interest group that has urged the enactment of sexual psychopath laws. He pointed out that many of the study committees have been composed largely or entirely of psychitrists. The statute enacted in Illinois was written by a committee of psychiatrists and neurologists, and the committee considering the question in Indiana received from the American Psychiatric Association copies of all such laws previously passed in other states. Sutherland pointed out, however, that "many prominent psychiatrists have been forthright in their opposition to [such laws]. They know that the sexual psychopath cannot be defined or identified. Probably most of the psychiatrists in the nation have been indifferent to legislation; they have exerted themselves neither to promote nor to oppose enactment."[11]

Definitions

Two facts become clear after a brief examination of statutory definitions of terms such as "sexual psychopath." Most of the definitions are vague or circular, and they add little to our understanding of what kinds of people are intended to be confined under these laws. Second, the definitions reveal substantial borrowing from one another, with the same phrases appearing over and over in different statutes. This borrowing is attributable to two factors—the "fad" that led to widespread adoption of such statutes at approximately the same time, and court decisions upholding specific language, which was then picked up in later enactments.

One of the most important cases in influencing the wording of sexual psychopath definitions is *Minnesota ex rel. Pearson* v. *Probate Court*, 309 U.S. 270 (1940), in which the U.S. Supreme Court adopted the Minnesota Supreme Court's construction of the definition of "psychopathic personality" and found it sufficiently precise to prevent the invalidation of the law as unconstitutionally vague and indefinite. The Minnesota court had construed the statute to apply to "those persons who, by an habitual course of misconduct in sexual matters, have evidenced an utter lack of power to control their sexual impulses and who, as a result, are likely to attack or otherwise inflict injury, loss, pain or other evil on the objects of their uncontrolled and uncontrollable desire."[12] This language appears in the Massachusetts, Oregon, Vermont, and District of Columbia statutes.

Table 2-1 quotes the full definition for each statute and also lists the offenses covered and the length of the commitments.

Table 2-1
Sexual Psychopath Statutes

Statutory Definitions	Offenses Included	Procedure	Length of Commitment
Alabama—Sexual Psychopath A person who is suffering from a mental disorder but is not mentally ill or feeble minded to an extent making him criminally irresponsible for his acts, which mental disorder having existed for a period of not less than one year and being coupled with criminal propensities to the commission of sex offenses.	Any sex offense. (Criminal code does not specify clearly which offenses are sex offenses.)	Conviction required	"Until fully and permanently recovered."
California—Mentally Disordered Sex Offender Any person who by reason of mental defect, disease, or disorder, is predisposed to the commission of sexual offenses to such a degree that he is dangerous to the health and safety of others.	*Required application:* misdemeanor sex offenses involving children under 14 if defendant has a previous conviction of a sex offense, all felony sex offenses involving children under 14. *Discretionary application:* any criminal offense "if it appears to the court that there is probable cause for believing such person is a mentally disordered sex offender."	Conviction required	Indeterminate
Colorado—Sex Offenders Act Commitment is allowed if the subject is a sex offender and the court finds beyond a reasonable doubt that the defendant constitutes a threat of bodily harm to members of the public.	Rape, gross sexual imposition, deviate sexual intercourse by force, deviate intercourse by imposition, sexual assault, sexual assault on a child, corruption of minors, seduction, aggravated incest, or attempt at any of these offenses.	Conviction required	One day to life.

Connecticut A person convicted of a crime who may be imprisoned at the Connecticut Correctional Institute (1 year or more) or a person convicted of a sex crime involving physical force or violence, disparity of age between adult and minor or a sexual act of a compulsive or repititive nature whom the court finds to be mentally ill, mentally deficient or emotionally unbalanced so as to demonstrate clearly such actual danger to society as to require custody, care or treatment.	Any offense for which punishment is imprisonment in the Connecticut Correctional Institute for 1 year or more; sex offenses involving physical force or violence, disparity of age between an adult and a minor or a sexual act of a compulsive or repetitive nature.	Conviction required	Not to exceed length of sentence authorized for offense.
Florida—Mentally Disordered Sex Offender A person who is not insane but who has a mental disorder and is considered dangerous to others because of a propensity to commit sex offenses.	Any offense.	No conviction required	Until court determines that he is recovered to a degree that he will not be a menace to others.
Georgia No definition. (Provides for examination of prisoners serving sentences for certain offenses to determine whether they have "any mental, moral or physical impairment which would render release inadvisable.")	Rape, assault with intent to rape, sodomy, kidnaping of a female by a male, incest, molesting children to gratify a sex urge.	Conviction required	One year, with one-year extensions allowed after further court action.
Illinois—Sexually Dangerous Persons All persons suffering from a mental disorder, which mental disorder has existed for a period of not less than one year immediately prior to the filing of the petition hereinafter provided for, coupled with criminal propensities to the commission of sex offenses, and who have demonstrated propensities toward acts of sexual assault or acts of sexual molestation of children.	Any offense.	No conviction required	Until recovered.

Table 2-1 (cont.)

Statutory Definitions	Offenses Included	Procedure	Length of Commitment
Indiana—Criminal Sexual Deviant Any person over the age of sixteen (16) years who has been convicted of a sexual offense or an offense which directly involved the commission of an illegal sexual act, and who is suffering from a mental disorder or defect which is coupled with a manifest tendency for the commission of sexual offenses, and has been determined treatable by the department of mental health.	Any sex offense, or any offense directly involving the commission of an illegal sexual act. Does not apply to forcible rape or misdemeanor sex offenses by first offenders. Applies to the following only if committed by force, violence or coercion or if a participant is under 16; abortion, bigamy, adultery and fornication, seduction, sodomy, homosexuality. Therefore mainly applicable to statutory rape, homosexual assault or other sexual assault not amounting to rape, and to seduction of persons under 16. Also includes some prostitution offenses, such as procurement, which are felonies.	Conviction required	No longer than maximum term for offense. Not more than two years unless treatment is producing improvement.
Iowa—Criminal Sexual Psychopaths All persons charged with a public offense who are suffering from a mental disorder and are not a proper subject for the schools for the mentally retarded or for commitment as a mentally ill person, having criminal propensities toward the commission of sex offenses and who may be considered dangerous to others.	Any public offense.	No conviction required	Until subject has received maximum benefit of treatment, and release will not be incompatible with the welfare of society.
Kansas Commitment is allowed if examination shows that the defendant is in need of psychiatric care and treatment and that such treatment can materially aid in his rehabilitation and that the defendant and	Any offense.	Conviction required	Maximum term allowed for offense, or until medical director finds that defendant is not dangerous and has received maximum benefit of treatment, whichever is less.

society are not likely to be endangered by permitting the defendant to receive such care and treatment in lieu of imprisonment.

Maryland—Defective Delinquent

Definition	Offense		Sentence
An individual who, by the demonstration of persistent aggravated antisocial or criminal behavior, evidences a propensity toward criminal activity, and who is found to have either such intellectual deficiency or emotional unbalance, or both, as to clearly demonstrate an actual danger to society so as to require such confinement and treatment, when appropriate, as may make it reasonably safe for society to terminate the confinement and treatment.	Felonies; misdemeanors punishable by imprisonment in the penitentiary; crimes of violence; sex offenses involving force or violence, disparity of age between an adult and a person under 18 or a sexual act of uncontrolled or repetitive nature; two or more convictions for offenses punishable by imprisonment.	Conviction required	Indeterminate

Massachusetts—Sexually Dangerous Person

Definition	Offense		Sentence
Any person whose misconduct in sexual matters indicates a general lack of power to control his sexual impulses, as evidenced by repetitive or compulsive behavior and either violence, or aggression by an adult against a victim under the age of sixteen years, and who as a result is likely to attack or otherwise inflict injury on the objects of his uncontrolled or uncontrollable desires.	Indecent assault; indecent assault and battery; indecent assault and battery on a child under 14; rape; rape of a female under 16; carnal knowledge and abuse of a female under 16; assault with intent to commit rape; open and gross lewdness and lascivious behavior; incest; sodomy; buggery; unnatural and lascivious acts with another or with a child under 16; lewd, wanton and lascivious behavior; indecent exposure; attempt at any of these offenses. Also applicable to any person under sentence in any correctional facility, including youth services, regardless of offense.	Conviction required	Indeterminate

Minnesota—Psychopathic Personality

Definition	Offense		Sentence
The existence in any person of such conditions of emotional instability, or	No offense required	—	Indeterminate

Table 2-1 (cont.)

Statutory Definitions	Offenses Included	Procedure	Length of Commitment
impulsiveness of behavior, or lack of customary standards of good judgment, or failure to appreciate the consequences of his acts, or a combination of any such conditions, as to render such person irresponsible for his conduct with respect to sexual matters and thereby dangerous to other persons.			
Minnesota—Sex Offenders Act No definition.	*Mandatory examination:* Aggravated rape; rape; sodomy; intercourse with a female under 16; indecent liberties; incest; attempt to commit aggravated rape, sodomy, intercourse with a female under 16. *Discretionary examination:* bestiality, leaving state to avoid establishment of paternity, prostitution, fornication.	Conviction required	Until expiration of sentence, or for one year, whichever is greater, subject to five-year extensions after court review.
Missouri—Criminal Sexual Psychopaths All persons suffering from a mental disorder and not insane or feeble minded, which disorder has existed for a period of not less than one year immediately prior to the filing of the petition, coupled with criminal propensities to the commission of sex offenses, and who may be considered dangerous to others.	Any offense.	No conviction required	Not specified; presumably indeterminate.
Nebraska—Sexual Psychopath Any person who has been convicted of a sex offense and who by the procedures of this section is determined to be disposed to repeated commission of sexual offenses which are likely to cause substantial injury to the health of others.	Debauching a minor, forcible rape, statutory rape, sodomy, any offense in which sexual excitement of the person committing the crime is a substantial motivating factor.	Conviction required	Until no longer a sexual psychopath.

New Hampshire—Dangerous Sexual Offender Any person suffering from such conditions of emotional instability or impulsiveness of behavior, or lack of customary standards of good judgement or failure to appreciate the consequences of his acts or a combination of any such conditions, as to render such person irresponsible with respect to sexual matters and thereby dangerous to himself or others.	*Mandatory application:* deviate sexual relations, corruption of minors, rape except where female is under 15 and consents, attempt at any of these. *Discretionary application:* incest, rape where female is under 15 and consents, more than one conviction for lewdness or indecent exposure, attempt at any of these.	Conviction required	Until court finds subject no longer dangerous to himself or others.
New Jersey—Treatment of Sex Offenders Treatment required for: one convicted of any of the specified offenses, whose conduct is found to be characterized by a pattern of repetitive, compulsive behavior, and violence or age disparity was indicated.	Rape; carnal abuse; sodomy; incest; private lewdness; open lewdness; indecent exposure; impairing the morals of a minor; attempt at any of these; assault with intent to commit rape, carnal abuse or sodomy.	Conviction required	Indeterminate, limited by maximum sentence authorized for offense.
Ohio—Psychopathic Offender Any person who is adjudged to have a psychopathic personality, who exhibits criminal tendencies and who by reason thereof is a menace to the public. Psychopathic personality is evidenced by such traits or characteristics, inconsistent with the age of such person, as emotional immaturity and instability, impulsive, irresponsive, reckless and unruly acts, excessively self-centered attitudes, deficient powers of self-discipline, lack of normal capacity to learn from experience, marked deficiency of moral sense or control.	*Mandatory application:* forcible rape; statutory rape, sexual battery; felony corruption of a minor between 12 and 15 by an offender 4 or more years older than victim; importuning (soliciting sexual activity from someone known to be unwilling or from a child under 13 or from a person under 18 if the offender is 4 or more years older); voyeurism; felony endangering of children; conviction of abusing, beating, torturing, starving or otherwise causing physical injury to a child. *Discretionary application:* any felony or misdemeanor where it has been suggested or appears to the court that the offender is mentally retarded or is a psychopathic offender.	Conviction required	Indeterminate

Table 2-1 (cont.)

Statutory Definitions	Offenses Included	Procedure	Length of Commitment
Oregon—Sexually Dangerous Person One, not insane, who by a course of repeated misconduct in sexual matters has evidenced such lack of power to control his sexual impulses as to be dangerous to other persons of the age of 12 or under because he is likely to attack or otherwise inflict injury or pain on the objects of his desire.	No offense required	—	Not specified; presumably indeterminate.
Tennessee—Sex Offenders No definition	Any offense involving the unlawful sexual abuse, molestation, fondling, or carnal knowledge of a child of 14 or under.	Conviction required	Until dangerous propensities no longer exist.
Utah—Mental Examination Before Sentencing Commitment is provided for persons convicted of certain sex offenses "if . . . it appears . . . that the person convicted suffers from any form of abnormal or subnormal mental illness, or other psychosis, which caused the commission of the sex offense."	Rape; sodomy; incest; indecent exposure; attempt at any of these; assault with intent to commit sodomy; indecent assault on a child; taking indecent liberties with a child.	Conviction required	For life, unless paroled or pardoned.
Vermont Psychopathic personality—those persons who by a habitual course of misconduct in sexual matters have evidenced such a lack of power to control their sexual impulse that they present a substantial risk of injury to others. Defective delinquent—a person who is a mental defective (retarded and requiring	Any felony, third conviction of any misdemeanor.	Conviction required	Indeterminate.

supervision for his own welfare or that of the community), who commits or has committed a criminal offense. (The statute apparently applies to "persons who, because of mental deficiency or psychopathic personality, violate the criminal laws of the state or are guilty of gross immoral conduct.")			
Washington—Sexual Psychopath Any person who is affected in a form of psychoneurosis or in a form of psychopathic personality, which form predisposes such person to the commission of sexual offenses in a degree constituting him a menace to the health and safety of others. Psychopathic personality—the existence in any person of such hereditary, congenital or acquired condition affecting the emotional or volitional rather than the intellectual field and manifested by anomalies of such character as to render satisfactory social adjustment of such persons difficult or impossible.	Abduction, incest, rape, assault with intent to commit rape, indecent assault, contributing to the delinquency of a minor involving sexual misconduct; sodomy; indecent exposure, indecent exposure, indecent liberties with children, soliciting or enticing child for immoral purposes, vagrancy involving immoral or sexual misconduct, attempt at any of these.	No conviction required	"Until, in the superintendent's opinion, he is safe to be at large."
Wisconsin—Sex Crimes Law Commitment is provided for persons convicted of certain sex offenses "if the department recommends specialized treatment for his mental or physical abberrations."	*Mandatory application:* rape, sexual intercourse without consent, indecent behavior with a child, attempt at any of these. *Discretionary application:* any other sex offense (including any offense except homicide if the court finds that defendant was probably motivated by desire for sexual excitement).	Conviction required	One year, or maximum sentence for offense.

Table 2-1 (cont.)

Statutory Definitions	Offenses Included	Procedure	Length of Commitment
Wyoming Conduct of the person has in the past been characterized by a pattern of repetitive or compulsive behavior accompanied either by: 1) violence, or, 2) an age disparity from which it shall appear that at the time of the crime . . . the victim was under 15 years of age and the convicted person was an adult aggressor.	Indecent exposure; rape; attempted rape; incest; sodomy; taking indecent liberties with a child; knowingly committing an immoral, indecent or obscene act in the presence of a child; causing or encouraging a child to commit or attempt to commit with defendant any immoral or indecent act; accosting, annoying or molesting a child with intent to commit an unlawful act.	Conviction required	Indeterminate, but limited to length of maximum sentence for offense. (A one-year limit is imposed for commitments of persons convicted of indecent exposure.)
District of Columbia–Sexual Psychopath A person, not insane, who by a course of repeated misconduct in sexual matters has evidenced such lack of power to control his sexual impulses as to be dangerous to other persons because he is likely to attack or otherwise inflict injury, loss, pain, or other evil on the objects of his desire.	No offense required. (If used in criminal cases, statute applies to persons charged with any offense except rape or assault with intent to rape.)	No conviction required.	Until sufficiently recovered so as not to be dangerous to other persons.
Pearson (construction of the Minnesota Supreme Court of the Psychopathic Personality Act as adopted by the Supreme Court). Those persons who, by an habitual course of misconduct in sexual matters, have evidenced an utter lack of power to control their sexual impulses and who, as a result,	—	—	—

55

are likely to attack or otherwise inflict
injury, loss, pain or other evil on the
objects of their uncontrolled and
uncontrollable desire.

In spite of the *Pearson* decision, and others finding such definitions sufficiently definite to survive constitutional challenge (see pp. 84-89), the definitions do not appear to provide useful guidance to a decision-maker faced with the question of whether to commit a specific subject. For example, the Connecticut statute refers to persons "whom the court finds to be mentally ill, mentally deficient or emotionally unbalanced so as to demonstrate clearly such actual danger to society as to require custody, care or treatment." The Indiana statute speaks of persons with "a manifest tendency for the commission of sexual offenses." The Florida definition includes any person who "is considered dangerous because of a propensity to commit sex offenses." The Maryland statute applies to persons who "clearly demonstrate an actual danger to society so as to require such confinement and treatment, when appropriate, as may make it reasonably safe for society to terminate the confinement and treatment."

All this language seems to resolve itself into the question, how dangerous is dangerous? If the subject is dangerous, he may be committed. To determine whether he is, the court must decide whether he ought to be committed. A similar reasoning process seems required under the Maryland definition: the subject is dangerous if he needs confinement and treatment in order not to be dangerous. The Florida language muddies the waters further by referring not to persons who are dangerous, but rather to persons who are *considered* dangerous. This may be even more difficult to determine.

The ambiguities of such definitions appear to reflect, in some degree, the lack of consensus among psychiatrists as to the meaning of such terms as "psychopath," "sociopath," and the more modern term "character disorder." Kittrie cited some of the disagreements:

"Even within psychiatry," psychiatrist Seymour Halleck noted recently, "there is widespread disagreement as to whether psychopathy is a form of mental illness, a form of evil or a form of fiction." Yet the law provides an elaborate system for the control of diverse types of deviants defined as psychopaths or defective delinquents.

"Psychopath" is one of the most criticized words in the psychiatric vocabulary. Its etymological definition is "a sick mind" although in medical usage it connotes not psychosis, neurosis, or mental defect, but rather a moral or social inadequacy. Some forty years ago Dr. William A. White, an early leader in the field of criminal psychiatry, declared that psychopathy had become a wastebasket diagnosis. The American Psychiatric Association has defined the psychopath as "a person whose behavior is predominantly amoral or antisocial and characterized by impulsive irresponsible actions satisfying only immediate or narcissistic interest . . . accompanied by minimal outward evidence of anxiety or guilt." Notwithstanding this impressive battery of scientific language, the association notes that the term is considered poor and inexact by many members.

Some psychiatrists strongly assert that the concept as well as the term is devoid of meaning. "[T]he term 'psychopathic personality' is no longer regarded by psychiatry as meaningful; yet it will probably remain embalmed for some time to come in the statutes of several states where the pursuit of demons disguised as sexual psychopaths affords a glimpse of a 16th Century approach to mental illness," commented one prominent psychiatrist. But Dr. Cleckley, an intensive researcher of psychopathic case histories, establishes an effective case for the psychopathic denomination and lists sixteen characteristics common to the class, including such desirable character traits as unusual charm and absence of irrational delusions but also such personality defects as unreliability, lack of remorse, pathological egocentricity, and poor interpersonal relations. The psychopath is thus seen as one who suffers not from a particular identifiable defect but as a person whose thinking, feeling, and acting are impaired by a disability of social interaction and responsibility.[13]

Legal difficulties with the use of such standards are reflected in case analysis of the meaning of the medical and psychological terms used in statutes and of their exact legal consequences. For example, in *Sas* v. *Maryland*, 295 F. Supp. 389 (D. Md., 1969), after lengthy consideration of the Maryland definition and of previous cases, the court adopts the following construction, quoting from a previous opinion in the same case.

. . .We conclude that in the light of the testimony in this case there is no need to give any further medical description to the nonmedical term "emotional unbalance" and that *if the matter is ever squarely before the Court of Appeals* [emphasis in original] that Court will conclude that the term "psychopath" is not a synonym for emotional unbalance, but that the term "emotional unbalance" as used in the Act refers to a medically recognized psychiatrically disordered person, who demonstrates "persistent aggravated anti-social or criminal behavior," and who exhibits a type of psychiatric disorder manifested by deep-seated emotional conflicts which distort the individual's attitude toward society, and of society's attitude, toward him, resulting in an uncontrollable desire and need to create continual hostile acts toward society and which is uncontrollable by the individual.

The court then rules that the statutory definition is not unconstitutionally vague.[14]

Despite the lack of precision of statutory definitions, it is possible to discern a number of elements that appear regularly, although in differing combinations. Twenty-two of the twenty-seven statutes in effect have a definition of some type. Seventeen definitions include mention of dangerousness or violence; fourteen include an element of propensities toward the commission of sex offenses; two mention propensities toward commission of other offenses; fourteen include an element of mental abnormality of some type, but not sufficient to relieve the subject of criminal responsibility under the insanity defense; and eight include the related element of compulsive or repetitive behavior or the lack of ability to control behavior. In addition, three include a requirement that the mental abnormality have continued for a specified period, usually a year, before proceedings are begun.

Offenses Included

Of the twenty-seven sexual psychopath statutes in effect, nineteen require the conviction for a specified offense before commitment proceedings can begin. Five (Florida, Illinois, Iowa, Missouri, and Washington) allow such proceedings upon a charge of a specified offense. Three others do not require criminal charges.[c] Five statutes have two-tiered application; if the subject is charged with any of one group of offenses, commitment proceedings are required; if he is charged with any of the second group, the court or the prosecutor can decide whether to begin proceedings.

Table 2-1 includes lists of the offenses covered by each sexual psychopath statute. Table 2-2 breaks down the offenses into twelve categories to illustrate the statutes' application to sex offenses, violent offenses, and other types of offenses.

The discussion of statutory definitions indicates the concern of many statutes with the danger of sex offenses. This concern is again reflected in the offenses to which such statutes apply. Fourteen of the statutes apply only to persons who have committed sex offenses.[d] Seven statutes are applicable to any offense;[e] three others are applicable to any felony and also include some misdemeanors.[f] No statute limits its coverage to violent offenses, and no statute even limits its coverage to serious offenses.

The concentration on sex offenses brings under these statutes' coverage a number of kinds of offenses that may be trivial as well as nonviolent. Since a number of states still have criminal prohibitions of certain sex acts between consenting adults, and even between married couples, a large number of the offenses included in sexual psychopath statutes are consensual acts. They would include prostitution offenses, in addition to homosexual activity and oral or anal sexual activity between adults of opposite sexes. Table 2-2 illustrates that every statute covers at least some consensual offenses, and almost all cover at least some minor sex offenses, such as indecent exposure.

Every statute now in effect does include both violent sex offenses and seduction or sexual enticement involving children. In addition, two include the category of "sexual imposition," which refers to various types of offensive sexual contact.[15]

cThe Minnesota Psychopathic Personality statute operates exactly like a civil commitment statute in the sense that any "reputable person" may file a petition alleging that the subject is a psychopathic personality, even though no criminal charges have been filed. Similarly, the Oregon statute requires no offense. The District of Columbia statute allows commitment proceedings to begin either when the subject has been charged with a specified offense, or when there is no criminal charge.

dAlabama, Colorado, Georgia, Indiana, Massachusetts, Minnesota (Sex Offenders Act), Nebraska, New Hampshire, New Jersey, Tennessee, Utah, Washington, Wisconsin, and Wyoming. The Massachusetts statute also applies to any person under sentence in any correctional institution, regardless of offense; with respect to persons examined immediately following the offense, only sex offenses are included.

eCalifornia, Florida, Illinois, Iowa, Kansas, Missouri, and Vermont.

fConnecticut, Maryland, and Vermont.

It can be concluded that such statutes throughly cover violent sex offenses and sex offenses involving children, the two kinds of sex offenses that arouse the most public concern. The usefulness of the statutes, however, is decreased by their inclusion of so many offenses that do not pose any threat or personal injury.

Two classes of included sex offenses that are of particular interest with respect to the purposes of sexual psychopath laws are "a sexual act of a compulsive or repetitive nature" (Connecticut and Maryland), and "any offense in which sexual excitement of the persons committing the crime is a substantial motivating factor" (Nebraska and Wisconsin). The repetitive or compulsive act is mentioned more often in definitions than among included offenses; it often refers to repeated incidents of indecent exposure. Both categories relate to the assumption that sex offenders proceed from minor offenses to serious ones, and that the lack of ability to control one's behavior is both an important identifying factor and a justification to confine sexual psychopaths.

A great deal of litigation has centered on the degree of danger posed to society by compulsive acts such as exhibitionism or by property offenses such as burglary, which are included in a number of statutes. In *Sas* v. *Maryland*, 295 F. Supp. 389 (D. Md., 1969), which arose under Maryland's Defective Delinquent Statute, the court considered in detail "whether the interpretation and application of the statutory requirement that a defective delinquent be found to be 'an actual danger to society' may within the eighth amendment's prohibition against cruel or unusual punishment include those whose conduct indicates no more than a danger to property rights as distinguished from violence to the person." The district court had been directed to consider this question on remand from the Fourth Circuit, and noted in its opinion some suggestions from the higher court. The court said that "it is impossible to 'draw any hard and fast line between damage to property and danger to individual, damage to a person'. . . . Likewise, the burglar is a prime risk of injury to person, particularly as to sex crimes, such as rape. The 'breaking and entering' associated with property, is easily transferred to the female body. Moreover, a property offense—a breach of the law—can easily lead to willingness to break another law—an offense to the person."[16]

After recounting expert testimony to the same effect, however, the court concluded that the statute was in fact being applied only to those persons found to pose a threat of offenses against the person and had not been construed to apply to those "whose conduct indicates no more than a danger to property."[17]

The question of the danger to persons posed by the chronic exhibitionist is addressed in *Millard* v. *Harris*, 406 F.2d 964 (D.C. Cir., 1968), in which the court considered in detail the kind of woman or child who was likely to witness such acts, and the psychic injury that unusually sensitive women or children might suffer from observing such acts.[18] The *Millard* court found the danger posed even by repeated acts of indecent exposure insufficient to justify the indeterminate commitment of the offender in the case. We do not know how

Table 2-2
Offenses Included

	Any offense	Any sex offense	Violent sex offenses	Sexual imposition	Sex offenses involving children	Consensual sex offenses
Alabama		X				
California	Xa				X	
Colorado			X	X	X	X
Connecticut			X		X	X
Florida	X					
Georgia			X		X	X
Illinois	X					
Indiana			X		X	X
Iowa	X					
Kansas	X					
Maryland			X		X	X
Massachusetts	b		X		X	X
Minnesota (PP)	No offense required.					
Minnesota (SOA)			X		X	X
Missouri	X					
Nebraska			X		X	X
New Hampshire			X		X	X
New Jersey			X		X	
Ohio			X	X	X	Xa
Oregon	No offense required.					
Tennessee					X	
Utah			X		X	X
Vermont						
Washington			X		X	X
Wisconsin		Xa	X	X	X	
Wyoming			X		X	X
D.C.	No offense required.c					

The category of "consensual sex offenses" includes such behavior as fornication, adultery, homosexual activity and sodomy, or other prohibited sexual conduct between married persons or adults of opposite sexes. The category of "minor sex offenses" includes such offenses as indecent exposure, voyeurism, prostitution, soliciting, or patronizing a prostitute.

aDiscretionary application.

bAlso applicable to any person under sentence in an correctional facility.

cAlso can apply in any offense except rape or assault with intent to rape.

Minor sex offenses	Nonsexual with sexual motivation	Any felony	Violent felonies	Other felonies	Other misdemeanors
X		X			
X		X			X
X					
	X				
X					
X					
X					
X					
		X			
X					
	X[a]				
X					

often sexual psychopath statutes are used in cases involving such conduct; however, as illustrated by Table 2-1, indecent exposure remains prominent among included offenses in a number of states.

Procedure

Procedure under sexual psychopath statutes ranges from the most sketchy outline, setting out little more than the authorized dispositions and not mentioning the subject's rights, to extremely complex plans, listing in detail all the subject's rights, time limits for examinations, reports, and decision-making, requirements of information to be included in medical reports and to be taken into account in decisions, and following up on commitments by requiring regular reports from the mental institution, listing the times at which the subject may petition for release, and providing detailed procedures for conditional discharge and disposition of remaining criminal charges.

The question of whether a particular sexual psychopath statute is classified as a criminal or civil statute is very important in determining the kinds of due process rights that must be afforded to subjects. A number of court rulings have turned on this issue, concluding that if a statute is criminal in nature, the subject is entitled to all the usual protections afforded to criminal defendants—including the right against self-incrimination, the right to appointed counsel, the right to a jury trial, the right to confrontation, evidentiary rules prohibiting use of hearsay, and proof beyond a reasonable doubt—before commitment may be ordered. If the proceeding is found to be a civil commitment, however, most of these rights are not constitutionally required (see pp. 89-96).

Alan Dershowitz described the civil-criminal issue as a "labeling game":[19]

The object of the civil-criminal labeling game is simple: the court must determine whether certain procedural safeguards, required by the Constitution in "all criminal prosecutions," apply to various proceedings. The rules are a bit more complex. The legislature enacts a statute that restricts the liberty of one player—variously called the defendant, patient, juvenile ward, deportee, et cetera. That player must then convince the court that the formal proceeding through which the state restricts his liberty is really a criminal prosecution. The state, on the other hand, must show that the proceeding is really civil; for support it often claims that the results of the proceeding help, rather than hurt, its opponent.

In the course of this game's long history, prosecutors have succeeded with the help of the court, and all too often, without the opposition of "defense" attorneys, in attaching the civil label to a wide range of proceedings including commitment of juveniles, sex psychopaths, the mentally ill, alcoholics, drug addicts, and security risks. Likewise, sterilization, deportation, and revocation of parole and probation proceedings are regarded as civil. By attaching this label, the state has successfully denied defendants almost every important safeguard required in criminal trials. Invocation of this talismanic word has erased a veritable bill of rights. As Alice said, "That's a great deal to make one word [do]." To which Humpty Dumpty responded: "When I make a word do a lot of work like that . . . I always pay it extra." Until quite recently, this word must have been well paid indeed, for it was doing the work of an army of jurists.[20]

Dershowitz further pointed out: "As with most traditional games, a number of favorite gambits have developed over the years. Some courts, for example, give no reason at all for concluding that a proceeding is civil. They simply assert, often in italics, that it is *clearly, demonstrably,* or *manifestly* civil."[21] Some courts attach conclusive significance to the part of the state statutes in which the proceeding appears. In *People* v. *Chapman,* 301 Mich. 584, 4 N.W.2d. 18 (1942), the Michigan Supreme Court found that the sexual psychopath proceeding was not criminal because it was not located in either the code of criminal procedure or the penal code. Other courts, however, have held statutes to be criminal even though not located in the criminal code, or they have held statutes to be civil even though the statutes were found in the criminal code.

Again, according to Dershowitz:

In accordance with Supreme Court dicta that evidence of a legislative intent to regulate rather than punish might justify the absence of criminal safeguards, courts sometimes look to the declared legislative purpose to decide whether a proceeding is civil or criminal. Thus, one state supreme court attributed significance to a statutory declaration that "the Director of the Department of Corrections shall engage in a program of research in the detention, treatment and rehabilitation of narcotic addicts." The court omitted to mention that similar hortatory statements decorate the pages of many penal codes. Some courts have gone as far as attributing significance to the title borne by the judicial document that commences the proceeding. As the California Supreme Court once observed: "The certificate [filed in this addict commitment case] is entitled 'The People of the State of California *For the Best Interest and Protection of Society and [the person to be committed]'* rather than 'The People v. the accused.' "[22]

Other courts have simply compared the proceeding in question to other, "clearly civil" proceedings to reach the conclusion that they are dealing with a civil statute. Dershowitz stated:

Another approach that courts sometimes use to justify their conclusion that a particular proceeding is civil suffers from as much circularity as these comparisons, but is far more dangerous. Courts sometimes reason that whether a proceeding is criminal or civil depends on the procedural safeguards that accompany it. If it has the safeguards usually associated with a criminal proceeding, then it is criminal; if it lacks those safeguards, then it must be civil . . . . The dangers of this approach are patent: it may actually encourage a state to eliminate important safeguards in order to assure that courts will regard the proceeding as civil. An episode from the history of Michigan's sex psychopath law demonstrates this danger.[23]

The Michigan sexual psychopath law that Dershowitz mentioned was enacted in 1937. In 1938 the state supreme court declared it unconstitutional, relying on placing the statute in the criminal code and also on due process requirements of the statute. As Dershowitz explained:

[I]n declaring the law unconstitutional, the court focused on two of the act's most important safeguards—the requirement of a specified sex offense conviction and the availability of jury trials on the issues of conviction and committability. The message to the legislature was clear: a constitutional sex psychopath law must eliminate the requirement of a conviction, do away with the right of two jury trials, and be published in the proper section of the code.

The following year the Michigan legislature did precisely that.... A man who had been charged with "an act of gross indecency" soon challenged his commitment under the new statute. This time, however, the court was

satisfied that the present statute ... contains none of the constitutional infirmities of the previous statute.... The present statute is not contained in either the Code of Criminal Procedure or the Penal Code. It makes sex deviators subject to restraint because of their acts and condition, and not because of conviction and sentence for a criminal offense. The procedure under this statute resembles a statutory inquest for the commitment of an insane person ....

Accordingly, the court held that the statute was civil and that the constitutional safeguards claimed by petitioner—protection against cruel and unusual punishment, self-incrimination, and ex post facto laws—did not apply.[24]

In recent years the importance of the civil-criminal distinction has been somewhat decreased by decisions requiring certain criminal-type protections in proceedings denominated as civil.[25] Table 2-3 lists the placement of each statute in the state's code and shows what the statute says about whether it is civil or criminal.

Sexual psychopath statutes are usually brought into play after the defendant has been convicted of a specified offense but before he is sentenced. The criminal proceedings are suspended while the psychiatric examination and legal determination are made; if the defendant is committed, the commitment is in lieu of a criminal sentence. Usually, after the defendant has completed treatment and has been discharged from the mental institution, no further action can be taken on the criminal charges. This procedure seems to comport with the claims of therapeutic beneficent purposes which are frequently made for such statutes, rather than punitive intent.[26] Under some statutes, however, the subject is returned to the trial court after discharge from the treating institution, and the court has discretion to impose a criminal sentence or to release him. In some but not all statutes of this type, the court is required to grant credit against the sentence for the time the subject has spent in therapeutic confinement.

As noted previously, in several states (Florida, Illinois, Iowa, Missouri, Washington, District of Columbia) the sexual psychopath statute applies to persons who have been charged with criminal offenses but not yet convicted. In a few other states the statute can be invoked while the subject is serving a prison term. For example, the Georgia statute requires the subject to be examined sixty days before his parole or other release from prison. The Massachusetts statute

Table 2-3
Civil and Criminal Sexual Psychopath Statutes

State	Location in Statutes	Nature as Indicated in Statute
Alabama	Criminal procedure	Criminal
California	Welfare and institutions code	–
Colorado	Separate part of criminal procedure section	–
Connecticut	Humane and reformatory agencies	–
Florida	Criminal procedure	Civil
Georgia	Board of pardons and paroles	Criminal, but commitment described as civil-type proceeding
Illinois	Criminal law and procedure	Procedure declared to be civil in nature
Indiana	In "Miscellaneous" part of title on criminal procedure	–
Iowa	Social welfare and rehabilitation	–
Kansas	Criminal procedure	–
Maryland	Separate section	–
Massachusetts	With mental health statutes	–
Minnesota (PP)	Probate code	–
Minnesota (SOA)	Public institutions	–
Missouri	Public health and welfare	–
Nebraska	Criminal procedure	–
New Hampshire	Public safety and welfare	–
New Jersey	Criminal procedure	–
Ohio	Criminal procedure	–
Oregon	Mental health (mentally ill and sexually dangerous)	–
Tennessee	Mentally ill and retarded persons	–
Utah	Criminal procedure	–
Vermont	Health and mental health	–
Washington	Separate chapter, next to civil commitment and alcoholism sections	–
Wisconsin	Sex crimes	Criminal
Wyoming	Criminal procedure	–
District of Columbia	Criminal offenses	–

can be invoked to apply to any person confined in a correctional institution, and the District of Columbia statute can be invoked while the subject is on probation.

In almost every state either the court or the prosecutor or both can invoke the sexual psychopath statute. In a few states (California, Colorado, Connecticut, Florida, Indiana, Massachusetts, Nebraska) the defendant can invoke the act. Table 2-4 shows when and by whom each statute can be invoked.

The Decision-Making Process

After a sexual psychopath statute is invoked, the first requirement is that the subject be given a psychiatric examination. A few states do not specifically require such an examination, but their statutes imply that it is clearly contemplated. Most statutes specify who is to make the examination, although a few merely speak in terms of a court inquiry into the subject's physical and mental state. In eleven states the examination is made by the staff of a state mental hospital, a special institution for examination and treatment of sexual psychopaths, or a state mental health department. In ten states the examiners are court-appointed consultants, at least one of whom must be a psychiatrist. In two states the court may choose either the institutional staff or consulting experts. In three states the statute requires only that the examiners be physicians.

In eight states the subject must be committed to an institution for his examination. In eleven more, such a commitment is allowed at the court's discretion. Two states provide for confinement in jail.

The statutes include very little information about the nature of the examination. Only eleven statutes provide time limits, ranging from 45 to 120 days, with 60 and 90 the most common. In other states the length of time allowed for the examination is left to the court's discretion, either explicitly or by implication. The Maryland statute provides specifically that the examiners are allowed as much time as they deem necessary to complete their examination and arrive at a diagnosis, and the state's position has been that Patuxent Institution is legally authorized to hold a subject in custody even past the expiration of the sentence imposed if a diagnosis has not been reached because of the subject's refusal to cooperate with the examiners. (This issue was litigated in *McNeil* v. *Director*, 407 U.S. 245 (1972), which will be discussed later.)

In twenty-four states the examiners are required to provide a written report to the court. In three more states the examiners may testify in lieu of presenting a formal written report, or the information may be provided by some other means.

Most of the statutes do not address the defendant's rights before and during the psychiatric examination. Given the nature of the decision on commitment, the information obtained from the subject during the examination and the examiners' opinions as to his mental state will be the most important factors in determining whether the subject will be committed. For this reason a number of due process issues are beginning to be raised both in sexual psychopath cases and in civil commitment cases, which have been the standard against which sexual psychopath procedures have been measured most often.

Table 2-4
Invocation of Sexual Psychopath Statutes

State	When Invoked	By Whom Invoked
Alabama	After conviction, before sentencing	Prosecutor or attorney general
California	After conviction, before or after sentencing	Trial court on own motion, on motion of prosecutor or an affidavit on behalf of defendant
Colorado	After conviction, before sentencing	Prosecutor, defendant, or court
Connecticut	After conviction, before sentencing	Court, prosecutor, or defendant
Florida noncapital crime capital crime	After charge After conviction	Court, prosecutor, or defendant
Georgia	60 days before parole or prison release	Chairman of state board of pardon and parole
Illinois	After charge	Attorney general or state's attorney
Indiana	After conviction, before sentencing	Prosecutor, court, or defendant
Iowa	After charge	Prosecutor, on own initiative or on receiving information from any reputable person
Kansas	After conviction, as part of presentence investigation	In discretion of court
Maryland	After sentencing, and any time up to 6 months before release from prison	Not specified
Massachusetts	After conviction, before sentencing; also, during confinement in prison	Court, on own motion, or on motion of prosecutor (prosecutor may act for prisoner or director of institution)
Missouri	After charge	Prosecutor
Nebraska	After conviction, before sentencing	Court; or prosecutor if psychiatric report given probable cause
	(Defendant may invoke act after charge, if psychiatric report gives probable cause)	
New Hampshire	After conviction, before sentencing	Court
New Jersey	After conviction, before sentencing	Court (referral apparently required for specified offenses)
Ohio	After conviction, before sentencing	Court
Minnesota PP	No criminal charge required	County attorney, if convinced by allegations of others
Minnesota SOA	After conviction, before sentencing	Court
Oregon	No criminal charge required	District attorney

Table 2-4 (cont.)

State	When Invoked	By Whom Invoked
Tennessee	After sentencing, after commitment to penal institution	Required upon conviction
Utah	After conviction, before sentencing	Court
Vermont	After conviction, before sentencing	Court, prosecutor, or commissioner of mental health
Washington	After charge	Prosecutor
Wisconsin	After conviction, before sentencing	Court (examination required for some offenses, discretionary for others)
Wyoming	After conviction, before sentencing	Court (referral required, unless court states reasons for not making referral)
District of Columbia	Before trial, or after conviction but before sentencing, or while subject is on probation (if criminal charge is filed)	U.S. attorney; any criminal court may direct prosecutor to file petition

One of these issues is the Fifth Amendment privilege against self-incrimination. It has been argued that the subject is entitled to this right, and that to protect it he is entitled to advice of counsel during psychiatric interviews, or at minimum that he should be informed before the interview that the information he provides to the examiners may be used to justify depriving him of his liberty.

Only five statutes specifically grant the right to counsel before the examination. Five also require that the subject be given notice of his rights before the examination. (None of these mention notice of the right not to talk to the examining physicians; they speak in terms of rights to counsel, rights to a hearing, and the like.) Only Colorado's statute says specifically that the subject has the right not to talk to the examiners. Five statutes say that he is required to cooperate, and four of these provide contempt penalties for refusal to do so.

In six states the subject has a statutory right to an independent psychiatric examination by a doctor of his own choice. In five of these the examination may be conducted at state expense if the subject is found to be indigent.

Under nineteen of the twenty-seven statutes, a recommendation by the examiners that the subject does not fall into the definition or does not need treatment is conclusive, and the sexual psychopath proceedings must be terminated. In this case the criminal proceedings, if any, against the subject will be continued. Six statutes do not specifically indicate the effect of such a negative conclusion by the examiners. In two states such a conclusion does not prevent further inquiry but merely serves as evidence in the determination.

In sixteen states the only effect of a psychiatric report indicating that the subject does fall within the class defined is to authorize a hearing or further inquiry. Most of the statutes, however, make clear that great weight is to be given to expert testimony. Some do so explicitly; in others the medical testimony is the only kind of evidence the statute mentions. Six statutes do not indicate the effect of a positive recommendation. In five states the examiners' conclusions appear to be controlling. In two of these (Georgia and Utah) a custodial commitment is required, and in the other three (New Jersey, Tennessee, and Wisconsin) the court has discretion to order either commitment or outpatient treatment.

Of the statutes that do not provide for conclusive decisions by examiners, six state that the subject is entitled to a jury trial on the issue of whether he falls within the statutory definition; if no jury trial is requested, the court will decide. A handful of the remaining states specify that the subject is not entitled to a jury trial, and the rest indicate only that the court makes the decision.

Once the defendant is found to fall within the statutorily defined group subject to commitment, a further question remains: whether commitment is mandatory or is left to the court's discretion. Five statutes give the court discretion to choose between custodial and outpatient treatment. In 8 states the court has wider discretion: to commit the subject, to release him, or in the case of subjects who are criminal defendants, to sentence him to a prison term or to probation. Twelve states require a commitment for custodial care. Table 2-5 shows who decides whether the subject falls within the class defined by statute, and whether commitment is required for all persons in the class.

Along with other information, Table 2-1 shows the length of commitments authorized under sexual psychopath statutes. The majority are wholly indeterminate, providing for release when the subject no longer falls within the statutorily defined class or when he is found to be no longer dangerous. A few are limited by the maximum sentence authorized for the offense involved, and a few have fixed time limits of one or two years.

Indeterminate confinement is one of the distinguishing characteristics of sexual psychopath statutes; it indicates that the medical model is in play. Where the length of the deprivation of liberty is not proportioned to the seriousness of the offense in question, the argument follows that the confinement is therapeutic rather than punitive; the subject is being incarcerated until he has been "cured" of his illness or of his dangerous propensities, not until he has atoned for a wrong or paid his debt to society. This very lack of proportionality, however, is one of the elements of such statutes that has been challenged repeatedly; a number of cases take the view that a confinement that is potentially for life is neither appropriate nor justifiable when it is premised on behavior that neither threatens nor causes injury to persons, although it may outrage sensibilities.[27] The constitutional and ethical implications of the indeterminate commitment will be considered later in this chapter.

Table 2-6 divides the statutes according to whether commitment is manda-

Table 2-5
Classification Decisions

State	Decision-Maker	Nature of Commitment
Alabama	Court	Mandatory
California	Court	Discretionary
Colorado	Court	Mandatory
Connecticut	Court	Mandatory
Florida	Court	Mandatory
Georgia	Examiners	Mandatory
Illinois	Jury or court	Mandatory
Indiana	Court	Discretionary
Iowa	Jury or court	Discretionary
Kansas	Court	Discretionary
Maryland	Jury or court	Mandatory
Massachusetts	Court	Either commitment or out-patient treatment required
Minnesota PP	Court	Discretionary
Minnesota SOA	Court	Either commitment or out-patient treatment required
Missouri	Jury or court	Not specified
Nebraska	Jury or court	Not specified
New Hampshire	Court	Mandatory
New Jersey	Examiners	Either commitment or out-patient treatment required
Ohio	Court	Discretionary
Oregon	Court	Discretionary
Tennessee	Examiners	Either commitment or out-patient treatment required
Utah	Examiners	Mandatory
Vermont	Court	Mandatory
Washington	Jury or court	Mandatory
Wisconsin	Examiners	Either commitment or out-patient treatment required
Wyoming	Court	Discretionary
District of Columbia	Court (jury possible, but court makes decisions)	Mandatory

tory or discretionary for persons found to fall into the statutorily-defined group. The table also lists the length of commitments. Commitments are indeterminate in ten of the twelve statutes with mandatory commitments, three of the five that require a choice between commitment and outpatient care, six of the eight with discretionary commitments, and both of the two that do not specify whether commitments are required.

Many of the statutes are vague on a number of procedural points. For example, seventeen say specifically that the subject, or his attorney, is entitled to access to all medical and psychiatric reports. Ten do not specify whether he may inspect them. Only three indicate clearly that he is entitled to other documents involved in the determination, such as presentence reports, probation reports, and welfare reports.

Fifteen statutes guarantee the right to counsel; in another five statutes the right is implied or would follow from the fact that the proceedings are characterized as criminal. In thirteen of the twenty states specifically guaranteeing counsel, the statute specifies or implies that counsel would be appointed for indigent subjects. Only a handful of states, however, indicate in exactly what situations the subject is entitled to the assistance of counsel, or at what point in the proceedings counsel would be appointed. A few speak of counsel "from the commencement of proceedings" or "at every stage in the proceedings"; others mention counsel only in the context of formal hearings.

Rules of evidence are of special concern, since many proceedings to determine mental condition, such as civil commitment hearings, routinely allow hearsay evidence. Hearsay is being increasingly challenged as an inappropriate or insufficient basis for a decision concerning deprivation of liberty.[28] Sexual psychopath statutes say very little about what kinds of evidence are admissible and what kinds should be provided. Eighteen make no mention of rules of evidence. The Colorado statute says the rules of evidence shall be the same as in criminal trials. Others say that "any other evidence that tends to indicate that he is a sexually dangerous person," will be competent (Massachusetts); that competent evidence as to prior conduct tending to show the existence of sexual psychopathy will be admissible (Nebraska); that evidence of prior sex acts or crimes and previous punishment will be admissible (New Hampshire); or that evidence of prior convictions tending to show that the defendant is a sex psychopath will be admissible (District of Columbia). Few of the statutes describe what kind of evidence must be considered aside from the medical reports. A few require probation department reports or social welfare reports.

Nor do many of the statutes specify what burden of proof the state must meet to justify confining a subject for treatment. The Nebraska and Colorado statutes require proof beyond a reasonable doubt that the subject falls into the specified class, and the Illinois statute has been so construed in recent cases (see p. 97. Oregon requires clear and convincing evidence. The other statutes that mention the question merely say that "the court shall ascertain" whether the subject falls within the class (Alabama); "that if the court finds" the subject to be a member of the class he may be committed (California, Massachusetts, Minnesota Psychopathic Personality, Ohio, and Vermont); or that "if [the subject] is found to be" a member of the class he may be committed (Washington). The Missouri statute says that the state must present prima facie evidence that the subject is a criminal sexual psychopath; again this does not indicate what burden of proof is required.

Table 2-6
Categories of Commitments

	Mandatory Commitments
Alabama	Until fully and permanently recovered
Colorado	One day to life
Connecticut	Not to exceed length of sentence authorized for offense
Florida	Until court determines that subject is recovered to a degree that he will not be a menace to others
Georgia	One year, with one-year extensions allowed after further court action
Illinois	Until recovered
Maryland	Indeterminate
New Hampshire	Until court finds subject no longer dangerous to himself or others
Utah	For life, unless paroled or pardoned
Vermont	Indeterminate
Washington	"Until, in the superintendent's opinion, he is safe to be at large"
District of Columbia	Until sufficiently recovered so as not to be dangerous to other persons

	Either Commitment or Outpatient Treatment Required
Massachusetts	Indeterminate
Minnesota SOA	Until expiration of sentence, or for one year, whichever is greater; subject to five-year extensions after court review
New Jersey	Indeterminate, limited by maximum sentence authorized for offense
Tennessee	Until dangerous propensities no longer exist
Wisconsin	One year, or maximum sentence for offense

	Discretionary
California	Indeterminate
Indiana	No longer than maximum term for offense; not more than two years unless treatment is producing improvement
Iowa	Until subject has received maximum benefit of treatment and release will not be incompatible with the welfare of society
Kansas	Maximum term allowed for offense, or until medical director finds that defendant is not dangerous and has received maximum benefit of treatment, whichever is less
Minnesota PP	Indeterminate
Ohio	Indeterminate
Oregon	Not specified; presumably indeterminate
Wyoming	Indeterminate, but limited to maximum sentence for offense.

Table 2-6 (cont.)

	Not Specified
Missouri	Not specified; presumably indeterminate
Nebraska	Until no longer a sexual psychopath

Several statutes involve a two-step commitment process. Some provide for a temporary commitment (following a psychiatric examination and court determination) and then a further medical review and a court decision on final commitment. Others require a medical review following the final commitment, with the option to modify the commitment order if institutionalization no longer seems appropriate. The states with two-step statutes are California, Indiana, Minnesota (Psychopathic Personality), Nebraska, and Ohio.

Appeal procedures are not clearly spelled out. In fact, fourteen of the twenty-seven statutes do not mention appeal, although clearly there would be some method of challenging a commitment, whether through the state's general appeal procedures or through a petition for release or for habeas corpus. The Indiana statute, which does not mention appeal, specifies that the right to habeas corpus is preserved in criminal sexual deviant proceedings. Five statutes specify a right to appeal as in criminal cases, and one describes the appeal as civil. In six other states the nature of the appeal is not specified.

Most of the statutes say little about what is expected to happen to the subject after the commitment, except for indicating the length of the commitment. In almost every state the subject is to be confined and treated either in a state mental hospital, a hospital for the criminally insane, or a special institution maintained for diagnosing and treating sexual psychopaths, such as Patuxent Institute in Maryland. The commitment, however, is often to the department of public welfare, the department of mental health, or the department of institutions, which in turn designates the appropriate facility. In a few states the commitment is to the department of corrections, which is expected to designate a correctional institution with psychiatric facilities.

The subject's exact status and rights while committed are rarely addressed. Twelve statutes make no mention of them at all, beyond a requirement of regular reports on the subject's condition. A few specify that the subject's rights are the same as those of civilly committed patients. This is true of the Minnesota Psychopathic Personality Statute, which in fact simply makes the state's civil commitment procedures applicable to persons with "psychopathic personality." Others, such as Alabama's statute, are drafted in terms of "complete authority" over the subject. The Minnesota Sex Offenders Statute states:

The commissioner [of public welfare] may irrespective of his consent require participation by him in vocational, physical, educational and correctional training and activities; may require such modes of life and conduct as seem best adapted to fit him for return to full liberty without danger to the public; and may make use of other methods of treatment and any treatment conducive to the correction of the person and to the prevention of future violations of law by him . . . . The commissioner may make use of law enforcement, detention, parole, medical, psychiatric, educational, correctional, segregative, and other facilities, institutions and agencies, public or private, within the state.

The commissioner is specifically authorized to transfer the subject freely between institutions for these purposes. The Wisconsin statute includes some similar language concerning control over committed subjects, but most statutes are not nearly so detailed.

The right to treatment, at least if the subject is found treatable, is guaranteed in Georgia, Nebraska, Tennessee, and in the Minnesota Psychopathic Personality Statute. The Minnesota Psychopathic Personality and Nebraska statutes require that individual treatment plans be devised.

Regular reviews of the status and condition of institutionalized subjects are required by fourteen of the twenty-seven statutes. Twelve of these require annual review, one requires review every six months, and one requires review every three years. Eleven statutes do not mention review, and in two others the commitment itself would require frequent court review.

Some of the statutes provide procedures under which the subject may bring a legal challenge to his continued confinement. In six states he may do so annually. In Missouri and Ohio, subjects may challenge confinement at any time. In Iowa they may do so at any time, provided that three psychiatrists appointed by the superintendent conclude that they are recovered. In Maryland no such challenge may be made until the subject has been institutionalized for two years or for two-thirds of the sentence imposed, whichever is more, and then challenges are permitted every three years. In fourteen states such challenges are not mentioned, and in two others they are not relevant because of the length of the commitment.

Ten statutes authorize incarceration of the subject in correctional institutions under at least some circumstances.[g] Under some of these statutes,[h] subjects may be transferred to such institutions if they are found to be untreatable or found to be still psychopathic or dangerous after having received the maximum benefit of treatment. In others, such a transfer is left largely to the discretion of the department to which the subject is committed. In Colorado, transfer is authorized if it is found to be "in the best interest" of the subject and the public. In Nebraska the transfer requires court approval. Under the Ohio statute, if the Department of Mental Health and Mental Retardation fails to designate an institution because of a lack of facilities, the subject will be sent to the same penal facility as if he had been regularly sentenced. The Vermont statute appears to authorize confinement in a penal institution from

[g]Alabama, California, Colorado, Illinois, Minnesota (Sex Offenders Act), Nebraska, New Hampshire, Ohio, Vermont, and Washington.

[h]Alabama, California, and New Hampshire.

the beginning of the commitment. In Washington, if the subject is found to be a custodial risk or a hazard to other patients, he may be transferred to a prison with psychiatric facilities. In Alabama, Florida, and New Jersey, confinement in correctional facilities appears to be contemplated, but the statutes do not list the circumstances under which it is authorized. In addition, at least one state, Maryland, maintains a special treatment facility, which is properly characterized as a maximum security institution although it is operated by a treatment staff. All except three of the states allowing confinement in penal institutions require convictions before commitment. The three exceptions are Florida, Illinois, and Washington.

Almost every statute provides for some type of conditional release, with either the committing court or a special panel determining when such release should be granted and what conditions should be imposed. Authorized conditions usually include whatever, in the discretion of the releasing authority, will insure the safety of the community.

In most states it is more difficult for a committed sexual psychopath to obtain release or final discharge than it is for civilly committed patients to do so. Most civil commitment statutes have been construed to require a finding of dangerousness before a person may be committed; in most states, however, the hospital superintendent is empowered to release involuntary civil patients whenever he finds it appropriate, without prior notice to the court. Sexual psychopath statutes provide more elaborate procedures that must be followed before release. Only three give institution superintendents such unqualified power to release. In most cases the court is the releasing authority, and in several cases a hearing is required before release. Table 2-7 lists the standards for release, the releasing authority, and the procedure, if any, required before release.

A number of the statutes are unclear as to the disposition of criminal charges after a final discharge from a treatment program. In six states[i] further action on criminal charges is barred. In at least one of these the indictment or information is quashed; in some others the commitment is in lieu of sentence, and therefore discharge has the same effect as completion of a prison term. In several states—such as Maryland, Washington, and Wyoming—the committing court has discretion to place the subject on probation or to require him to serve a prison sentence, with credit given for the time spent in a mental institution.

Representative Statutes

Three sexual psychopath statutes will be described in detail to provide a better understanding of how the statutes operate and how they differ in provisions and scope. The Maryland Defective Delinquent Statute was chosen because it is so well known, and because it is an example of a broad sexual psychopath statute

---

[i]Colorado, Illinois, Indiana, Kansas, Massachusetts, and Minnesota (Sex Offenders Act).

Table 2-7
Release Procedures

State	Standard for Release	Releasing Official; Procedures
Alabama	Fully and permanently recovered	Director or superintendent of institution
California	Has received maximum benefit of treatment and is not a danger to the health or safety of others	Court, after hearing
Colorado	Release is in best interest of subject and society, and subject is not a threat of bodily harm	Parole board
Connecticut	Subject is no longer in need of custody, care or treatment	Court, after receiving a report from superintendent
Florida	Subject has recovered to the degree that he is no longer a menace	Court
Georgia	Subject has shown good conduct and efficient performance, will be law-abiding and will be able to employ himself	Pardon and parole board
Illinois	Subject has recovered	Court
Indiana[a]	Subject has recovered	Court, after hearing
Iowa	Subject has received the maximum benefit of hospitalization, and release is not incompatible with the welfare of society	Court, after hearing
Kansas[a]		
Maryland	Subject has sufficiently improved to warrant unconditional release from custody	Court, on recommendation of institutional board of review
Massachusetts	Subject is no longer a sexually dangerous person	Court
Minnesota PP	Subject can make an "acceptable adjustment to society	Superintendent of hospital on order of commissioner of public welfare, after favorable recommendation from special review board
Minnesota SOA[a]	There is reasonable probability that subject can be given full liberty without danger to public	Commissioner of public welfare

State	Criteria	Release authority
Missouri	Subject has improved to extent that discharge will not be incompatible with welfare of society	Court, after hearing
Nebraska	No longer sociopathic	Court
New Hampshire	Subject has recovered to the extent that he is no longer dangerous to himself or to others	Court
New Jersey	Subject able to make acceptable social adjustment	Parole board (discharge may be allowed only after a term on parole)
Ohio	Subject has recovered or improved sufficiently as to no longer require special care, custody, or treatment, and is no longer a danger to public	Court, on recommendation of department, and after hearing
Oregon	Subject is no longer a sexually dangerous person	Court
Tennessee	Subject's dangerous propensities no longer exist	Court, after hearing
Utah	Subject has sufficiently recovered from his mental illness to make repetition of sex offenses unlikely	Probation, parole, and pardon authority
Vermont	Subject is no longer a defective delinquent or sexual psychopath who is a threat to public welfare or is dangerous while at large	Court
Washington	Subject is safe to be at large	Court
Wisconsin	There is reasonable probability that subject can be given full liberty without danger to the public	Generally, department of health and social services; however, in less than two years without approval of the committing court
Wyoming	Release on parole if person is capable of making acceptable social adjustment in community	Committing court, on recommendation of hospital director
District of Columbia	Subject has sufficiently recovered so as not to be dangerous to other persons	Superintendent of hospital; if subject was charged with a crime, notice must be given to court

aStatute provides an absolute time limit on commitments; at the end of the authorized period, the subject must be released, regardless of the medical staff's assessment of his condition. There may be additional procedures allowing earlier release.

with wide coverage of offenses. The Indiana Criminal Sexual Deviant Statute, enacted in 1971, is included because it shows how narrowly a statute may be drafted to exclude minor offenses and to include statutory due process protections. A Kansas statute entitled "Deferring sentence pending mental examination," the successor to an earlier sexual psychopath statute, is described because it suggests an approach that may offer many of the stated benefits of sexual psychopath statutes without a complex statutory scheme.

Maryland

The Maryland statute is found in Article 31B, Ann. Code Md., entitled "Defective Delinquents." It establishes a governing board for Patuxent Institution within the Department of Public Safety and Correctional Services.[j] The board must include a professor of psychiatry from the University of Maryland, a professor of psychiatry from Johns Hopkins University, two sociologists from the University of Maryland and Johns Hopkins University, a professor of constitutional law from the University of Maryland, the state director of parole and probation, and two practicing attorneys, or substitutes designated by these persons.

Section 5 provides: "For the purposes of this article, a defective delinquent shall be defined as an individual who, by his demonstration of persistent aggravated antisocial or criminal behavior, evidences a propensity toward criminal activity, and who is found to have either such intellectual deficiency or emotional imbalance, or both, as to clearly demonstrate an actual danger to society so as to require such confinement and treatment, when appropriate, as may make it reasonably safe for society to terminate the confinement and treatment."

Requests for examination may be filed with respect to any person convicted and sentenced for a felony, a misdemeanor punishable by imprisonment in the penitentiary, a crime of violence or a sex crime involving physical force or violence, disparity of age between an adult and a person under eighteen, or a sexual act of uncontrolled or repetitive nature. The statute also applies to persons with two or more convictions for offenses punishable by imprisonment.[k]

---

[j]Located in Jessup, Maryland, Patuxent is an institution maintained exclusively for the examination, diagnosis, and treatment of defective delinquents.

[k]The following are defined as crimes of violence in 27 Ann. Code Md. 441(3): abduction, arson, burglary, escape, housebreaking, kidnaping, manslaughter (except involuntary manslaughter), mayhem, murder, rape, robbery, the attempt to commit any of these offenses, and assault with intent to commit any other offense punishable by imprisonment for more than one year.

Requests may be filed at any time after sentencing on a criminal charge, up to within six months of the expiration of the sentence imposed. They may be filed by the Department of Corrections, the prosecutor, or the defendant himself.

Once a request for examination is filed, the defendant must be committed to Patuxent for an examination, to be made by at least three staff members, including a physician, a psychiatrist, and a psychologist. Their written report is to be submitted, preferably within six months; in any event, it must be completed at least three months before the expiration of the defendant's sentence.[1] The defendant is entitled to an independent examination, and the state is to pay the "reasonable costs" of such examination.

If the Patuxent staff report states that the defendant is not a defective delinquent, he is returned to the corrections department to serve his sentence. If the report says that he is a defective delinquent, a court hearing is required for final determination of the issue. The defendant is entitled to notice and counsel, and counsel will be appointed if the defendant is indigent. The hearing must be held within thirty days of designation of counsel for the defendant, unless he requests a delay. Either the state or the defendant may request a jury trial; the jury decides whether the defendant is a defective delinquent.

If the defendant is found not to be a defective delinquent, he is returned to the corrections department to serve his sentence. If he is found to be a defective delinquent, the statute requires his commitment to Patuxent Institution for an indeterminate period. His criminal sentence is suspended during the time of his commitment. Either the defendant or the state may apply for leave to appeal a determination on the issue of defective delinquency. If an indigent defendant is granted leave to appeal, the state pays for a hearing transcript, and filing fees are waived. The right to petition for a writ of habeas corpus is specifically preserved.

After the inmate has been in Patuxent for two years, or for two-thirds of his sentence, whichever is *longer*, he may petition for a court review of whether he is still a defective delinquent. This review requires a hearing, substantially like the original court determination. If the court determines that the defendant is still a defective delinquent, he may petition for subsequent reviews at three-year intervals.

During the commitment, an institutional review is required every year; it is made by an institutional board of review composed of the director, the three associate directors, the University of Maryland law professor on the Patuxent board, both lawyers on the board, and a sociologist from a university in the

---

[1]The three-month limit was apparently added in response to *McNeil* v. *Director*; see p. 99. Before the Supreme Court's ruling in *McNeil*, the state's position had been that if a defendant who did not cooperate with the examining staff by providing the information they requested could be held indefinitely even if his sentence had expired. Uncooperative defendants now are charged with civil contempt and held in confinement under contempt citations even after their sentences have expired. See *Williams* v. *Director*, discussed on p. 97.

state, who is appointed by the Patuxent board. Written recommendations must be filed after each annual review. The board may grant parole or leave of absence of up to one year, on such conditions as it deems necessary. It may revoke parole or change the conditions at any time. It may allow release during working hours so that an inmate may hold a job. If this is done, the inmate's wages must be paid to the board, which pays the inmate's daily work expenses, deducts for the cost of his lodging and treatment, and holds the remainder for the inmate.

If the institutional board of review recommends unconditional release, it must inform the committing court. The court then conducts an inquiry, which may include a hearing. After the inquiry, the court may order unconditional release, conditional release on parole or leave of absence, or continued commitment. If it orders unconditional release, it may in its discretion return the inmate to the corrections department to serve the remainder of his sentence; credit, including reduction for good behavior, must be given for the time spent in Patuxent.

Indiana

The Indiana Criminal Sexual Deviant Statute is found in Indiana Code 35-11-3.1-1 et. seq. (formerly 9-4001 et. seq.).

The term "criminal sexual deviant" is defined to mean "any person over the age of sixteen (16) years who has been convicted of a sexual offense or an offense which directly involved the commission of an illegal sexual act, and who is suffering from a mental disorder or defect which is coupled with a manifest tendency for the commission of sexual offenses, and has been determined treatable by the department of mental health."

The act does not apply to persons convicted of the following offenses, unless committed by force, violence or coercion or unless a participant is under sixteen: abortion, bigamy, adultery and fornication, seduction, sodomy, and homosexuality. Further, the act does not apply to subjects convicted of misdemeanor sex offenses who have no previous convictions of sex offenses in Indiana or any other state.

A section enacted in 1974 prohibits application of the act in cases of forcible rape. Therefore the act applies mainly in cases of statutory rape or rape made possible by the victim's mental illness or lack of understanding, to homosexual assault or other sexual assault not amounting to rape, and to any type of seduction of persons under sixteen. Other sex offenses that are felonies include enticing a female for prostitution, enticing a female into immoral places for vicious or immoral purposes, and procuring for prostitution. Several misdemeanor sex offenses are on the books, such as prostitution, keeping a house of prostitution, and frequenting a house of prostitution or associating with prostitutes. The maximum penalties for these offenses are very short, however; only two range up to six months. In view of the act's prohibition of a commitment lasting longer than the maximum penalty for the crime committed, it appears impractical to invoke the act in misdemeanor prosecutions.

The crime of assault and battery includes certain kinds of sexual enticement and sex acts with children, which might be construed as separate crimes from those included in seduction or fornication involving a child under sixteen. Therefore the act could be applicable to those offenses, and it may also be applicable to public indecency, for which the penalty can be one year in prison if children are involved.

Petitions for a finding of criminal sexual deviancy are filed after conviction and before sentencing, and can be filed by the prosecutor, the court, the defendant, or a person acting on behalf of the defendant. Upon filing, the court must appoint two or three physicians, all but one of whom must be specialists in mental disorders, to examine the defendant.

The court must also authorize a probation officer to investigate the circumstances surrounding the crime and the previous record and history of the defendant. A copy of his report is sent to the examining physicians. The physicians' report is filed with the court, is open to inspection by the defendant and his counsel, and is inadmissible in any proceeding except a determination of criminal sexual deviancy or a civil commitment hearing.

The defendant is entitled to counsel "during his examination" by the physicians; this probably does not contemplate the presence of counsel during sessions with the physicians. If two of the examining physicians find the defendant "a probable criminal sexual deviant," the court sets a hearing for a determination that the defendant is a probable criminal sexual deviant. The defendant is entitled to have notice of the hearing, to have counsel, to call witnesses, and to cross-examine witnesses.

If the court finds that the defendant is probably a criminal sexual deviant, he must be committed to a state mental hospital for observation for not more than 120 days. Before the end of that time, the Department of Mental Health must file with the court a report stating whether the defendant is treatable, and if so, the approximate length of his treatment. This report is open to inspection by the defendant and his counsel, and is not admissible in any other proceeding except a civil commitment hearing, unless so requested by the defendant.

If the report states that the defendant is not a criminal sexual deviant or is not treatable, he is sentenced under the criminal statutes, and the time spent in the hospital under the temporary commitment is credited against any prison terms.

If the report states that the defendant is a criminal sexual deviant and that he is treatable, the court may make a determination of criminal sexual deviancy and commit the defendant to the Department of Mental Health "to be either confined in a state psychiatric institution or treated by an approved facility." Such a determination and commitment are not mandatory under the statute, however.

A commitment under this act cannot exceed the maximum sentence for the crime for which the defendant was convicted.

If the defendant has not recovered in two years and the superintendent of the institution believes that further treatment would be futile, the defendant is returned to the court for further disposition, and the time he spent while committed is credited against any prison sentence imposed.

While he is a committed patient, the defendant has "such privileges granted to other patients of the facility as are not incompatible with the person's care, supervision or treatment or unreasonably dangerous to the community." He must be examined at least once a year by at least one physician qualified to make a preliminary examination. The physician submits a report to the court, including "any facts tending to show appearance of recovery." This report is available to the defendant's counsel and can be used in a hearing on discharge.

The hospital superintendent may file a petition for discharge, and the court then holds a hearing. The criterion for discharge is whether the defendant has recovered. Discharge bars further incarceration for the crime of which the defendant was convicted.

If the Department of Mental Health believes that the defendant has not recovered when the maximum time of his commitment is about to expire and also believes that he meets the requirements for civil commitment, it can notify the prosecuting attorney of the county in which the defendant was convicted at least fifty days before the expiration of the commitment. The prosecuting attorney may then begin a civil commitment proceeding not less than thirty days before the expiration of the commitment.

The Department of Mental Health may release the defendant on parole "to such persons and under such conditions as his condition, in the judgment of the department, merits." A defendant receiving outpatient care may be confined by the department for failure to appear for treatment; he can be prosecuted for the commission of a crime while under the department's care.

The act contains a section specifically noting that nothing in the act shall be construed to preclude a petition for a writ of habeas corpus or the pursuing of any post-conviction remedy.

Kansas

The Kansas statute, found in Kan. Stat. Ann. 22-3429 to 22-3431, reads as follows:

Sec. 22-3429. Deferring sentence pending mental examination. After conviction and prior to sentencing and as part of the presentence investigation authorized by K.S.A. 1969 Supp. 21-4604, the trial judge may order the defendant committed to a state hospital or any suitable local mental health facility for mental examination, evaluation and report. If adequate private facilities are available and if the defendant is willing to assume the expense thereof such commitment may be to a private hospital. A report of the examination and evaluation shall be furnished to the judge and shall be made available to the prosecuting attorney and counsel for the defendant. A defendant may not be detained for more than 120 days under commitment made under this section.

Sec. 22-3430. If the report of the examination authorized by the preceding section shows that the defendant is in need of psychiatric care and treatment and that such treatment can materially aid in his rehabilitation and that the defendant and society is [sic] not likely to be endangered by permitting the defendant to receive such care and treatment in lieu of confinement or imprisonment, the trial judge shall have power to commit such defendant to any state or county institution provided for the reception, care, treatment and maintenance of mentally ill persons. The court may direct that the defendant be detained in such institution until further order of the court or until the defendant is discharged under 22-3431. No period of detention under this section shall exceed the maximum term provided by law for the crime of which the defendant has been convicted. The trial judge shall, at the time of the commitment, make an order imposing liability upon the defendant, or such person or persons responsible for the support of the defendant, or upon the county or the state, as may be proper in such case, for the cost of admission, care and discharge of such defendant.

The defendant may appeal from any order of commitment made pursuant to this section in the same manner and with like effect as if sentence to a jail, or to the custody of the director of penal institutions had been imposed in this case.

Sec. 22-3431. Disposition upon completion of treatment. Whenever it appears to the chief medical officer of the institution to which a person has been committed under section 22-3430, that such person is not dangerous to himself or others and that he will not be improved by any further detention in such institution, such person shall be returned to the court where he was convicted and shall be sentenced, committed, granted probation or discharged as the court deems best under the circumstances. The time spent in a state or county institution pursuant to a commitment under section 22-3430 shall be credited against any sentence confinement [sic] or imprisonment imposed on the defendant.

Summary

The Maryland statute vests great powers in the board and staff members of Patuxent Institution. It authorizes indeterminate commitments, and the provisions for requests for court review appear to contemplate long commitments. It applies to large numbers of offenders, not only sex offenders, but also recidivists of any kind. It authorizes commitments for offenders who may not be treatable, or who do not profit from treatment; these offenders may be held in Patuxent indefinitely. In addition, it creates the possibility that an offender who has been released from Patuxent after being declared cured of the condition that caused his criminal conduct may then be required to serve out a sentence imposed for that conduct.

The Indiana statute, on the other hand, carefully limits the length of confinements and also limits application to a small number of specified offenses. In fact, by excluding consensual sex offenses and very minor offenses, and by requiring a finding of treatability, it leaves very few offenders subject to commitment. Its procedural provisions are carefully drawn, and it requires two court decisions before the final commitment is ordered.

The Kansas statute seems to be an attempt to graft the treatment aspect of psychopathic offender statutes onto usual sentencing procedures. It applies to offenders convicted of any offense; as in the case of the Indiana statute, however, the limitation of the commitment to the maximum sentence for the offense means that it will be impractical to invoke the statute for those convicted of offenses with short sentences. Like the Indiana statute, it applies only to offenders who are found likely to profit from treatment. It does not, however, provide for follow-up on whether the offender is benefiting, nor does it require periodic reviews of the continued justification for the commitment.

As the discussion of constitutional issues will indicate, none of these three statutes is a wholly satisfactory answer to the problems they address. They do, however, illustrate the widely differing approaches that may be taken to those problems.

Constitutional Issues

Constitutional challenges to sexual psychopath statutes have been made repeatedly since the first of the statutes were passed in the 1930s. Except for a few cases in which entire statutory schemes were declared unconstitutional,[29] courts have rejected most of these challenges. In recent years, however, state courts have begun to construe the statutes to require some of the procedural protections of criminal prosecutions.

Constitutional challenges have asserted that the statutes violate rights in the following ways: they are vague and overbroad; they do not provide equal protection and due process; they impair the right to trial by jury; they deny the privilege against self-incrimination; they subject offenders to double jeopardy, and they allow the imposition of cruel and unusual punishment.

Because of the extent to which these issues overlap, it is difficult to distinguish among them carefully and discuss them one at a time. Court opinions often touch on several without making careful distinctions and without announcing the exact bases for their decisions. In addition, issues concerning procedural rights largely turn on whether statutes are construed to be civil or criminal. The issues of vagueness, overbroadness, and equal protection will be discussed first, then distinctions made between civil and criminal proceedings, and finally the specific procedural due process requirements.

The closely related issues of unconstitutional vagueness and overbreadth, and denial of equal protection, have been considered over and over in litigation involving sexual psychopath statutes. The author found no case in which a court has declared a sexual psychopath statute unconstitutional because the classification of a special group of offenders was found to violate equal protection, or the definition of the group so classified was held to be impermissibly vague.[m]

Major authority for the constitutionality of sexual psychopath classifications comes from *Minnesota ex rel. Pearson* v. *Probate Court*, 309 U.S. 270 (1940), which upheld the Minnesota Psychopathic Personality Statute. As indicated in the previous discussion, the U.S. Supreme Court found the statutory definition (see Table 2-1) as construed by the Minnesota Supreme Court, sufficiently definite to withstand constitutional challenge, thus approving language that has since been adopted in several other statutes. The court said:

This construction of the statute destroys the contention that it is too vague and indefinite to constitute valid legislation. There must be proof of a "habitual course of misconduct in sexual matters" on the part of the person against whom a proceeding under the statute is directed, which has shown "an utter lack of power to control their sexual impulses," and hence that they "are likely to attack or otherwise inflict injury, loss, pain or other evil on the objects of their uncontrolled and uncontrollable desire." These underlying conditions, calling for evidence of past conduct pointing to probable consequences are as susceptible of proof as many of the criteria constantly applied in prosecutions for crime. . . .

Equally unavailing is the contention that the statute denies appellant the equal protection of the laws. The argument proceeds on the view that the statute has selected a group which is a part of a larger class. The question, however, is whether the legislature could constitutionally make a class of the group it did select. That is, whether there is any rational basis for such a selection. We see no reason for doubt upon this point. Whether the legislature could have gone farther is not the question. The class it did select is identified by the state court in terms which clearly show that the persons within that class constitute a dangerous element in the community which the legislature in its discretion could put under appropriate control. As we have often said, the legislature is free to recognize degrees of harm, and it may confine its restrictions to those classes of cases where the need is deemed to be the clearest. If the law "presumably hits the evil where it is most felt, it is not to be overthrown because there are other instances to which it might have been applied" [citations omitted].[30]

The same issues were considered in a series of cases arising under the Maryland Defective Delinquent Statute. The cases are: *Sas* v. *Maryland* (*Sas* I), 334 F.2d 506 (4th Cir. 1964), *Director* v. *Daniels* (*Daniels* I), 238 Md. 80, 206 A.2d 726 (1965), *Director* v. *Daniels* (*Daniels* II), 243 Md. 16, 221 A.2d 397, cert. den. 385 U.S. 940 (1966), *Sas* v. *Maryland*, (*Sas* II), 295 F. Supp. 389 (1969), affd. sub. nom. *Tippett* v. *Maryland*, 436 F.2d 1153 (4th Cir., 1971),

[m]But *Millard* v. *Harris*, 406 F.2d 964 (D.C. Cir., 1968), which will be discussed on p. 86, did interpret the District of Columbia statute very narrowly in conjunction with the civil commitment statute, and it questioned whether the class so defined included any offenders at all.

cert. dismissed sub. nom. *Murel* v. *Baltimore City Criminal Court*, 407 U.S. 355 (1972). The first discussion was by the Fourth Circuit in *Sas* I, which said, "We hold that statute to be facially constitutional, i.e., it is within the power of the state to segregate from among its lawbreakers a class or category which is dangerous to the public safety and to confine this group for the purpose of treatment or for the purpose of protecting the public from further depredations."[31]

In *Daniels* II, the Maryland court reached the same conclusion, saying, in part, "that the state has the power to restrain the liberty of persons found to be dangerous to the health and safety of the community is clear if the restraint is founded upon a legislative enactment providing a definite and certain description of a recognized group of persons dangerous to the health and safety of the people which is susceptible of ascertainment by proof."[32] The court also found that there is a medically recognizable group that meets the statutory definition, and that lay people can identify them with the aid of expert testimony. It found the standard no more vague than the *M'Naghten* or *Durham* rules for the insanity defense nor than Maryland's civil insanity test.

In *Sas* II, the district court discussed in detail some questions raised by the Fourth Circuit in *Sas* I relating to the meanings of the terms "psychopath" and "emotionally unbalanced," and considered expert testimony on the issue. The district court quoted language from *Daniels* II:

. . . We conclude that in the light of the testimony in this case there is no need to give any further medical description to the nonmedical term "emotional unbalance"; and that *if the matter is ever squarely before the Court of Appeals* that Court will conclude that the term "psychopath" is not a part of the definition, is not a synonym for emotional unbalance, but that the term "emotional unbalance" as used in the Act refers to a medically recognized psychiatrically disordered person, who demonstrates "persistent aggravated anti-social or criminal behavior," and who exhibits a type of psychiatric disorder manifested by deep-seated emotional conflicts which distort the individual's attitude toward society, and of society's attitude toward him, resulting in an uncontrollable desire and need to create continual hostile acts toward society and which is uncontrollable by the individual. It was in this context, we feel, that the doctors were describing a particular type of individual when they used the term "psychopath" and it is in that context that the Court of Appeals used the term "psychopath . . ." [243 Md. 36-37, 221 A.2d 409; emphasis added].

The District of Columbia statute, with wording similar to the language upheld in *Pearson*, was declared constitutional in *Miller* v. *Overholser*, 206 F.2d 415 (D.C. Cir. 1953); the statutory definition was found to be sufficiently definite to be constitutional.

In 1968, the Court of Appeals for the District of Columbia Circuit again considered the validity of the definition of "sexual psychopath" under the District of Columbia statute, in *Millard* v. *Harris*, 406 F.2d 964 D.C. Cir. (1968). The statute defined a sexual psychopath as "a person, not insane, who by a course of repeated misconduct in sexual matters has evidenced such lack of power to control his sexual impulses as to be dangerous to other persons because he is likely to attack or otherwise inflict injury, loss, pain or other evil on the objects of his desire." The petitioner, who had been committed as a sexual psychopath on the basis of several incidents of indecent exposure, argued that enactment of the 1964 Hospitalization of the Mentally Ill Act [21 D.C. Code 501-491 (1967)] partially or wholly superseded the sexual psychopath statute. The issue centered on the precise meaning of the term "not insane" in the sexual psychopath statute. The court pointed out that when the sexual psychopath statute was passed in 1948, its language was explicable.

If an individual was "insane," he could be civilly committed; the commitment statute then in force spoke throughout in that language. And if a criminal defendant was "insane" at the time of his offense, the "insanity defense" would excuse him from punishment.

Nor was it then senseless to invoke the medical model and provide for the hospitalization of a class of persons who were not "insane." The tendency then still extant to equate that term to psychosis and a clear break with reality resulted in a large category of persons who were not "insane," but who needed and would profit from psychiatric treatment. This Court acknowledged as much when we first encountered the statute in 1953 and found it constitutional.[34]

The court reviewed the changing meaning of the terms "insane" and "mentally ill," especially in the context of the *Durham* rule,[35] and also considered the scope of the 1964 civil commitment act, which provided for hospitalization of the "mentally ill" rather than the "insane." It concluded that the term "mentally ill" encompassed a broader category and included persons whose condition would not qualify as "insanity" under the older statute. This meant that people who previously would have been eligible for commitment as sexual psychopaths because they were not "insane" but nevertheless suffered from mental conditions indicating a need for treatment would now fall under the civil commitment statute because they would be considered "mentally ill."

The court then considered how the 1964 civil commitment act affected the application of the sexual psychopath statute:

These developments in the law pose the question of what role remains for the Sexual Psychopath Act, if indeed that statute survives at all. On the level of policy, one might well conclude that the more flexible standards now applied in the areas of the insanity defense and civil commitments leave scant need for a separate statutory scheme for sexual offenders. While the world of the "not insane" might in 1948 have included many men for whom treatment within a mental institution was more appropriate than criminal punishment, the changes in substance and semantics since then have narrowed if not eliminated the class of offenders ineligible for civil commitment or the insanity defense but still too sick to deserve criminal punishment.[36]

The court, however, found no evidence of legislative intent for the 1964 civil commitment statute to supersede the sexual psychopath statute.

The opinion continued:

Today, however, we confront statutes providing for civil commitment if the person is "mentally ill, and because of that illness, . . . likely to injure himself or other persons," and for commitment as a sexual psychopath if the person is "not insane, . . . [but] by a course of repeated misconduct in sexual matters has evidenced such lack of power to control his sexual impulses as to be dangerous to other persons." Our earlier discussion has shown that the class of "mentally ill" persons, as that term is understood today, includes some disturbed individuals who would have been considered "not insane" at the time the Sexual Psychopath Act was enacted in 1948. But serious problems of equal protection would arise were we to conclude that the statutes permit the Government to commit these mentally ill persons under the Sexual Psychopath Act while all other mentally ill individuals are accorded the greater procedural protections incorporated in the 1964 Hospitalization of the Mentally Ill Act. . . . More important, perhaps, are the vast differences between the two statutes regarding release. . . .

It would indeed be strange logic to argue that the fact that a person is "mentally ill" but not so mentally ill as to be "insane" as the word was understood in 1948 justifies withholding from him the protections of the civil commitment law. Nor can we conceive of any rational reason for shading the procedural rights incident to commitment and release simply because the person's dangerous proclivities manifest themselves in the form of sexual misconduct.[37]

To avoid these equal protection problems, the court concluded that term "not insane" in the sexual psychopath statute must be construed to mean "not mentally ill."

However, the court found that this construction created a further problem with the statute, "as to whether its language is not so meaningless or self-contradictory as to be constitutionally infirm. Specifically, the problem is whether a person who by a pattern of repeated sexual misconduct has demonstrated himself sufficiently dangerous to meet that part of the statutory definition is not, as a definitional matter, mentally ill and therefore outside the statutory definition."[38] In spite of this doubt, the court held that a finding that no persons existed who could fit the definition would be too broad; it chose to maintain its policy of making case-by-case determinations of mental illness. Since the court found that the petitioner's past conduct did not establish the dangerousness required by the statute, it held that the definition did not apply to him, and did not reach the question of whether he was mentally ill.

The court added some further observations on the statute, as construed.

. . . [W]e begin with the premise that when "not insane" is read to mean "not mentally ill" the sole justification for commitment under the sexual psychopath statute is his dangerousness to others. Since that is true, we must view the statute realistically as one which borders close upon preventive detention—detention which under our statute does not even require prior conviction of a criminal act. [As noted on p. 54, the District of Columbia statute may be invoked with or without a criminal charge.]

When the statute is evaluated in that light, constitutional issues of the gravest magnitude immediately appear. Substantively, there is serious question whether the state can ever confine a citizen against his will simply because he is likely to be dangerous in the future, as opposed to having actually been dangerous in the past. Since a prediction of likely dangerousness can only be premised upon past behavior, there are closely related procedural questions concerning the proof of past conduct. When a person is being committed to a mental hospital not beause he is mentally ill but only because his past conduct allegedly demonstrates his likely dangerousness, we have great difficulty imagining how the full protection of the self-incrimination privilege and the right to confront and cross-examine witnesses could constitutionally be denied him.[39]

The court did not reach the issue of the exact procedural protections required, since it held that the statute did not apply to the petitioner.

The vagueness issue was considered more recently in *People* v. *Pembrock*, 62 Ill.2d 371, 342 N.E.2d 28 (1976), which upheld the Illinois Sexually Dangerous Persons Statute (see table 2-1). The court said:

A statute is unconstitutionally vague if the terms are so ill-defined that the ultimate decision as to its meaning rests on the opinions and whims of the trier of fact rather than any objective criteria or facts.... However, we find that sufficient objective criteria exist in the Act to meet constitutional requirements. As defendant concedes in his brief, under the Act the phrase "sexually dangerous person" requires proof of (1) a mental disorder in existence for at least one year, (2) propensities to the commission of sex offenses, and (3) demonstrated propensities toward acts of sexual assault or acts of sexual molestation of children.[40]

The next question is whether sexual psychopath statutes are properly characterized as civil or criminal.

In *U.S. ex rel. Gerchman* v. *Maroney*, 355 F.2d 302 (3rd Cir., 1966), Pennsylvania's Barr-Walker Act[41] was found to be penal in nature, and its procedures for indeterminate confinement were declared to violate the due process clause. The statute authorized confinement for offenders convicted of certain offenses[n] if they would otherwise "constitute a threat of bodily harm to members of the public" or they were mentally ill habitual offenders. The prisoner seeking release under a writ of habeas corpus asserted that the statute denied the right to indictment and the right to confront and cross-examine witnesses. The second claim rested on the fact that the committing court's ultimate conclusions were based on a confidential psychiatric report.

The state argued that the proceeding was a simple civil commitment for the defendant's benefit, or alternatively, that it was a sentencing hearing, in which the rights of confrontation and cross-examination would not apply. The court, however, found both the language and purpose of the act to indicate that it was a criminal statute: "It may be invoked only after a precedent conviction of guilt

---

[n]Indecent assault, incest, assault with intent to commit sodomy, sodomy, and assault with intent to ravish or to rape.

of one of the specified crimes and prescribes a new and radically different punishment."[42] The court did not find the periodic psychiatric evaluations under the parole board's auspices proof of the civil nature of the statute. ". . . [I]t is no less a criminal proceeding and no less the infliction of criminal punishment because the Act provides for such studies, especially when this is accompanied by the drastic potential of life imprisonment if they do not affirmatively provide a basis for release. This criminal punishment does not lose its characteristic because the Act goes beyond simple retribution."[43] After quoting from *U.S.* v. *Brown*[44] to the effect that punishment encompasses retributive, rehabilitative, deterrent and preventive elements, the court continued, "The effort of enlightened penology to alleviate the condition of a convicted defendant by providing some elements of advanced, modern methods of cure and rehabilitation and possible ultimate release on parole cannot be turned about so as to deprive a defendant of the procedures which the due process clause guarantees in a criminal proceeding."[45]

One of the best-known cases involving sexual psychopath statutes is *Specht* v. *Patterson*, 386 U.S. 605 (1967), in which the Supreme Court declared the Colorado Sex Offenders Act unconstitutional. The court said of the statute, "It makes one conviction the basis for commending another proceeding under another Act to determine whether a person constitutes a threat of bodily harm to the public, or is an habitual offender and mentally ill. That is a new finding of fact . . . that was not an ingredient of the offense charged. The punishment under the second Act is criminal punishment even though it is designed not so much as retribution as it is to keep individuals from inflicting future harm."[46] The *Specht* opinion, like *Gerchman*, referred to *U.S.* v. *Brown* in its analysis of the civil-criminal question. It likened the Colorado statute to habitual criminal laws that make recidivism a distinct issue in the proceeding, but that provide for procedural protections not available under the Sex Offenders Act.

It may be significant that the Pennsylvania statute struck down in *Gerchman* used the word "sentence" to refer to the indeterminate confinement that could be ordered. The Supreme Court in *Specht* also referred to a "sentence" rather than a "commitment."

The question of the civil or criminal nature of the Maryland Defective Delinquent Act was considered in the *Sas* and *Daniels* cases. The following material is summarized from the Fourth Circuit's description of the Maryland statute in *Sas* I (1964); parts of the description that duplicate the material on pp. 78-80 have been omitted.

The defendant is entitled to counsel and to jury trial, but the right to speedy trial does not apply. The state must establish by a preponderance of the evidence that the defendant is a defective delinquent. Expert witnesses are to be accorded very serious consideration. The experts of Patuxent Institution are not in a patient-physician relationship with the defendant, so he may not assert the privilege to prevent their testimony, even if it concerns previous criminal acts.

Extensive hearsay evidence is admitted since the purpose of the act would be defeated "unless evidence of antecedent conduct is presented upon which to establish the propensity toward criminal activity." The defendant's own psychiatrist is not in the position of a medical expert in an adversary proceeding; rather he is considered independent, and he is required to submit a report to the court. The defendant has no control over the admission of this report, and again the physician-patient privilege does not apply.

The defendant's counsel has access to Patuxent Institution reports and independent reports, and he may employ general civil discovery procedures.

The sole issue at the hearing is whether the defendant is a defective delinquent; the jury, as trier of fact, is precluded from considering whether treatment will aid the defendant or whether any treatment is available. If the defendant is released from Patuxent before the expiration of his criminal sentence, he may be required to serve it: "While it is clear that a Patuxent inmate is subject to immediate and actual physical confinement without maximum or minimum limits, there is no requirement that he be given treatment unless the same is 'appropriate.' "[47] The opinion goes on as follows:

It is obvious . . . from the statistics to date, that the justification for the Act may not rest solely or even primarily on the theory that all defective delinquents will receive treatment or that the majority of the inmates who do will be greatly benefitted or even cured by treatment. Certainly this is true for the foreseeable future unless unanticipated increases in staff and breakthroughs in the science of psychiatry make great changes in the amount and efficacy of diagnosis and treatment possible. Many of the inmates will, therefore, in all likelihood, be confined for life on the premise that they are untreatable or uncurable, but, nevertheless, too dangerous to be released in a free society.[48]

The question of whether the statute could be construed as civil was remanded by the Fourth Circuit in *Sas* I for reconsideration by the district court. The issue was considered in *Daniels* II before the district court reconsidered *Sas*, and the Maryland court concluded that the objectives of the act were being sufficiently implemented in practice to justify classifying the proceedings as civil. The court said:

. . . [O]nly if the statute is regulatory can the precise criminal procedures required to uphold the constitutionality of a penal statute be dispensed with. If, on the other hand, the act is regulatory and therefore civil in nature, the Fourteenth Amendment of the Constitution's requirement is met if there is provided reasonable safeguards [sic] under the circumstances which include consideration of the fact that persons may be deprived of their liberty for the good of society and themselves. It seems clear that if there exists affirmative evidence that the act results from a legislative intent to regulate rather than punish, the law is deemed to be civil in nature. *Kennedy* v. *Mendoza-Martinez*, 372 U.S. 144, ... (1963).[49]

The court then concluded that the legislative history of the act did reveal the necessary regulatory purpose. It also noted that other sexual psychopath statutes similar to the Maryland act had been construed to be civil. Based on.expert testimony that the statute as applied was in fact accomplishing its purposes, the court concluded that it could not say the statute was clearly ineffectual. Using the test of the act's effectiveness in accomplishing its aims, the court declared the statute civil.

In *Sas* II, the federal district court reached the same conclusion concerning the statute's nature. It provided a number of reasons for doing so:

1. The district court thought that the Fourth Circuit in *Sas* I had by implication found the statute to be civil by declaring the procedural protections of the act sufficient to satisfy due process. (The district court in *Sas* II considered the question of due process as required by the Sixth Amendment together with the civil-criminal question. Since the act does not provide the criminal due process protections that would be required by the Sixth Amendment, the district court seemed to assume that if the procedural protections are sufficient, then the statute must be civil.)

2. In *Daugherty* v. *State of Maryland*, 355 F.2d 803 (1969), the Fourth Circuit quotes from a Maryland decision that refers to the statute's civil nature.[50] The district court says of this quotation, "The apparent acquiescence of the Fourth Circuit panel two years after the *Sas* [I] decision in the constitutionality of the interpretation placed by the Court of Appeals of Maryland on the Act is highly significant, if not fully determinative."[51]

3. The district court found the reasons given by the Maryland Circuit Court, in holding the statute civil in *Daniels* II so convincing that it quoted them.[52] The Maryland court said in part:

We conclude from the evidence before us that the legislative history of the Defective Delinquent Act clearly demonstrates that its sole objective and purpose was not penal but an effort to segregate a known group of mentally disordered people who are found guilty of criminal acts, by confining them in an institution housing only members of their group in a sole effort to protect society and provide treatment to effect, if possible, a cure of the illness. From the history it is clear that the legislative imposition of sanctions by restraining the individual results from studies that indicate that such restraint is necessary both for the protection of society and to provide medical treatment to further curative measures. In short, it is the State's effort to determine the cause of a criminal's acts and if associated with mental disorder to accomplish improvement under psychiatric supervision so that he may hopefully be released, no longer a danger to himself or society. This act now before the Court is so similar in design and has a legislative purpose so similar to the act that was before the Supreme Court in Minnesota, ex rel. Pearson v. Probate Court, supra, that we believe the decision of that court upholding the constitutionality of the Minnesota Sexual Psychopath Law is direct authority for our conclusion that this act is civil in nature. We further point out that the purpose of this act is so closely akin to the so-called "Sexual Psychopath" laws enforced in some twenty (20) states and the District of Columbia, that the decisions of the Courts in those jurisdictions that each of their laws is civil in nature is [sic] ample authority to conclude that the Maryland Act is regulatory. State v. Madary, 178 Neb. 383, 133 N.W.2d 583 (1965); People v. Levy, 151 Cal. App. 2d 460, 311 P.2d 897 (1957); Miller v. Overholzer, 92 U.S. App. D.C. 110, 206 F.2d 415 (1953); In re Miller, 98 N.H. 107 95 A.2d 116 (1953). . . .[53]

The Maryland Court also applies the standards set out in *Kennedy* v. *Mendoza-Martinez*, and concludes as follows:

After considering these factors, we conclude that the statute on its face supports the conclusion that the act is civil in nature. We find this for the following reasons: Even though the sanction does involve an affirmative restraint it is provided only because it is deemed best for the protection of society and best for the protection and treatment of the individual that he be placed in a maximum security institution maintained solely for the defective delinquents and not for other members of the criminal element. Historically, this type of sanction or restraint to accomplish the purposes of the Act has not been regarded as punishment but regulatory and is more akin to those laws consistently held to be civil in nature applicable to the "sexual psychopaths." Also this is true of laws involving loss of liberty by restraint of many mentally ill persons in mental hospitals in all of the states. The Maryland Act does not come into play on a finding of "scienter," because the person involved must before referral for diagnosis already have been convicted of at least one criminal act and can be determined to be a "defective delinquent" only after there has been an intensive mental examination. The law on its face clearly shows that it was not enacted to promote the aims of punishment, retribution and deterrence, but its only purpose is for the protection of society, and the treatment of the individual to effectuate a cure if at all possible. The Act clearly demonstrates that "defective delinquency" is not a crime but is a mental condition that can only be diagnosed and determined to exist after a finding of guilt. There exist alternate purposes which are valid functions of the State as a part of its police power. They are the protection of society, coupled with a humanitarian attempt to treat, cure and rehabilitate those suffering from abnormal mental functioning. The sanctions or incarceration provided by the Act are not excessive in relation to these alternative purposes since most reputable psychiatrists agree that treatment cannot be related to a fixed period of confinement, as the length of time necessary for treatment and cure, if it can be obtained, is uncertain. In addition, experience has demonstrated that the indeterminate confinement is itself therapeutic, as it has a tendency to generate and motivate the individual to participate in the institutional program in order to help himself. . . .

We therefore conclude that the Maryland Defective Delinquent Act is civil in nature under either test; that is, such a conclusion results from the legislative history and also the Act on its face supports this finding after taking into account the tests laid down by the Supreme Court in *Kennedy*.[54]

While these cases do not provide an exhaustive survey of opinions construing sexual psychopath statutes as either civil or criminal, they do offer a fairly comprehensive discussion of the reasons usually offered for the decisions. (See p. 62 for Dershowitz's discussion of the civil-criminal question.)

Within the last few years, the issue has declined somewhat in importance, as courts have begun to rule that even though a statute may be civil, some procedural protections traditionally offered only in criminal proceedings are nevertheless required.[o] These decisions will be discussed on pp. 96-99.

Discussions on the civil or criminal nature of the statutes focus on whether sexual psychopath statutes operate to punish specific conduct, to restrain and treat people with certain mental abnormalities, or both. A further question is whether these purposes are permissible to the state. The Supreme Court has considered these questions in *Robinson* v. *California*, 370 U.S. 660 (1962) and *Powell* v. *Texas*, 392 U.S. 514 (1968), and these two cases offer some guidance, by analogy, on sexual psychopath issues.

In *Robinson* the court ruled that criminal conviction and punishment for being a narcotics addict constituted cruel and unusual punishment, because addiction was a condition, and any punishment at all for a condition or an illness was cruel and unusual. The same argument was urged on the court in *Powell*, with respect to a defendant, a chronic alcoholic, who was fined $20 for public drunkenness. The court found, however, that Powell had not been punished for the condition of alcoholism, but rather for the act of appearing in public in an intoxicated condition. The two cases offer some analysis of constitutional powers of states to deal with "conditions" and "offenses." *Robinson* involved a prosecution that the state had construed to be for the status of being a narcotics addict, and addicts could be prosecuted under the statute even if they had never used or possessed narcotics in California. In addition to making it clear that a status could not be criminally punished, Justice Potter Stewart's opinion listed other options for states. A statute requiring medical treatment, even involving involuntary confinement, or imposing penal sanctions for refusing treatment, would be legitimately within the state's police power to control narcotics, *Robinson* says.

It is unlikely that any State at this moment in history would make it a criminal offense for a person to be mentally ill, or a leper, or to be afflicted with a venereal disease. A State might determine that the general health and welfare require that the victims of these and other human afflictions be dealt with by compulsory treatment, involving quarantine, confinement, or sequestration. But, in the light of contemporary human knowledge, a law which made a criminal offense of such a disease would doubtless be thought to be an infliction of cruel and unusual punishment in violation of the Eighth and Fourteenth Amendments. . . .

We cannot but consider the statute before us as of the same category. In this Court counsel for the State recognized that narcotics addiction is an illness. Indeed, it is apparently an illness which may be contracted innocently or involuntarily. We hold that a state law which imprisons a person thus afflicted as a criminal, even though he has never touched any narcotic drug within the State or been guilty of any irregular behavior there, inflicts a cruel and unusual punishment in violation of the Fourteenth Amendment. To be sure, imprisonment for ninety days is not, in the abstract, a punishment which is either cruel

---

[o]These rulings are generally in line with juvenile cases such as *In re Gault*, 387 U.S. 1 (1966) and *In re Winship*, 397 U.S. 358 (1970).

or unusual. But the question cannot be considered in the abstract. Even one day in prison would be cruel and unusual punishment for the "crime" of having a common cold.[55]

Justice Tom C. Clark, dissenting, argued that the statute was therapeutic in purpose, even though it carried a penal sanction. The goals of the system, he said, were the treatment and rehabilitation of addicts and the prevention of further drug use. He argued that confinement of an addict need not be in a hospital to be therapeutic, and he concluded that the California scheme was precisely what the court had found permissible: a program of compulsory treatment requiring periods of involuntary confinement. He thought the issue discussed by the court was a meaningless quibble over whether the statute should be labeled penal or therapeutic.

Many of Clark's arguments, of course, have been advanced in support of sexual psychopath statutes. For example, *In re Maddox*, 351 Mich. 358, 88 N.W.2d 440 (1958), involved a defendant who had been charged with an offense (but not convicted), committed to a state hospital as a sexual psychopath, and then administratively transferred from the hospital to a state prison. Hospital officials had testified that when a patient was uncooperative or refused to admit the offenses he had been accused of, the best therapy was to transfer him to a prison until he could acquire self-discipline, and then return him to the hospital for further treatment. The Michigan Supreme Court, however, found no authority for confining an unconvicted defendant in a prison either on authority of a commitment order or of a transfer ordered by the hospital. Sexual psychopath statutes that permit committed patients to be transferred to prisons seem to rely on an argument similar to Justice Clark's: that penal incarceration can itself be therapeutic in some instances.

In *Powell*, the court considered whether the alcoholic defendant could control his behavior and refrain from the prohibited act. The court refused to accept the lower court's findings that a chronic alcoholic is powerless to control his drinking. It pointed out that there is no generally accepted definition of the term "alcoholic." The court did say, however, that *Robinson* does not stand for the proposition that a defendant may not be punished for being in a condition he is powerless to change.

The reasoning of *Robinson* offers support for the view that a state may constitutionally require confinement and treatment for sexual psychopaths, as long as punishment is not imposed for the condition of sexual psychopathy. *Powell*, on the other hand, suggests that a state may constitutionally punish a sexual psychopath for acts that his mental condition compelled him to commit. These cases, however, do not offer much guidance in determining when a confinement is punitive and when it is therapeutic. The language of *Robinson* suggests that use of the term "civil commitment" rather than "conviction" and "sentence of imprisonment" and confinement in a medical institution rather than a correctional one will go a long way toward justifying an involuntary confinement as therapy rather than punishment.

Now some cases on constitutionally required procedural protections will be considered. Since most of the statutes provide for notice and hearing, right to counsel, and appointed counsel for indigents, recent procedural cases have focused on the burden of proof and the privilege against self-incrimination.

The California Supreme Court considered the burden of proof in *People* v. *Burnick*, 14 Cal. 3rd 306, 121 Cal. Rptr. 488, 535 P.2d 352 (1975). This case involved a defendant who had been committed as a mentally disordered sex offender (MDSO) after being convicted of sex offenses involving boys aged thirteen and fifteen. The committing court had made its decision on the basis of the preponderance of the evidence, because the California statute specifies that civil rules of procedure are to be used. The court ruled that procedural issues were not settled by reliance on the general proposition that the proceedings are civil.

The opinion said, "In light of the fundamental similarity between the sexual psychopath proceedings challenged in *Specht* and in the case at bar, the question is whether proof beyond a reasonable doubt is among the 'full panoply of the relevant protections which due process guarantees in state criminal proceedings.'"[56] The court concluded that this question was answered by the reasoning of *In re Winship,*[57] which held that juveniles charged with delinquency were entitled to proof beyond a reasonable doubt. *Winship* gave two reasons for the reasonable doubt requirement in criminal cases: a criminal defendant is subject to loss of liberty, and he is also stigmatized by conviction. Since *Gault* had already shown that these same consequences flowed from a determination of juvenile delinquency, *Winship* ruled that the proof must be beyond a reasonable doubt.

In *Burnick*, the California court said that these reasons for the higher standard of proof also apply to MDSO proceedings. It noted that a psychiatrist had described Atascadero State Hospital, where MDSOs were confined, as looking more like a prison than a hospital, and that an MDSO's loss of freedom could be more severe and more lengthy than a juvenile delinquent's. The stigma and loss of good name suffered by a person declared to be an MDSO also was found to be at least as great as for juvenile delinquents. The court noted that at least one federal court has required the reasonable doubt standard in civil commitments.[58]

The opinion said:

The contrary arguments of the People are not persuasive. Running throughout the People's position is the view that the standard of proof beyond a reasonable doubt is not required because mentally disordered sex offender proceedings are "predictive in nature": i.e., inasmuch as the state is not trying to prove that the defendant committed a particular illegal act in the past but rather is "predisposed" to commit sex crimes in the future, fewer safeguards against factual error are required. The facile attractiveness of this theory, however, masks the weakness of its underlying assumption. The assumption is that predictive judgments are truly valid, and that the probability of error in such judgments is significantly less than the probability of error in judgments determining that specific past events occurred. As sometimes happens to our most cherished preconceptions, reality is otherwise.

In the light of recent studies it is no longer heresy to question the reliability of psychiatric predictions. Psychiatrists themselves would be the first to admit that however desirable an infallible crystal ball might be, it is not among the tools of their profession. It must be conceded that psychiatrists still experience considerable difficulty in confidently and accurately *diagnosing* mental illness. [emphasis in original]. Yet those difficulties are multiplied manyfold when psychiatrists venture from diagnosis to prognosis and undertake to predict the consequences of such illness. . . .[59]

The court said that the predictive nature of the decision in an MDSO proceeding reinforced its determination to require a higher standard of proof. It concluded that the commission of an offense might well depend on highly fortuitous circumstances, and for that reason, even a record of several previous offenses might not provide the basis for accurate prediction.

The court added further: "And because the major purpose of this rule is to overcome an aspect of those proceedings which 'substantially impairs the truth-finding function,' our decision today must be given complete retroactive effect." [citation omitted].[60]

Federal courts reached the same result with respect to the Illinois statute in *Stachulak* v. *Coughlin*, 369 F. Supp. 628 N.D. Ill., 1973, aff'd. 520 F.2d 931 (7th Cir. 1975) and by the Illinois Supreme Court in *People* v. *Pembrock*, 62 Ill. 2d 317, 342, N.E.2d 28 (1976). The *Pembrock* opinion quoted the Seventh Circuit opinion in *Stachulak:* "We recognize that society has a substantial interest in the protection of its members from dangerous deviant sexual behavior. But when the stakes are so great for the individual facing commitment, proof of sexual dangerousness must be sufficient to produce the highest recognized degree of certitude."[61]

The *Stachulak* ruling was given retroactive effect in *U.S. ex rel Morgan* v. *Sielaff*, 546 F2d. 218 (7th Cir., 1976), because the imposition of the higher standard of proof was held to be designed to cure a defect going directly to the heart of the truthfinding function of proceedings under the Illinois statute.

The issue of the Fifth Amendment rights of subjects of sexual psychopath proceedings was considered in *Williams* v. *Director, Patuxent Institution* Maryland Court of Appeals, 276 Md. 272, 347 A.2d 179 (1975). The case arose under the Maryland Defective Delinquent Act. Two offenders committed for examination under the statute refused to cooperate in diagnostic interviews and were cited for civil contempt. They were held under the contempt citations after their original criminal sentences had expired. They maintained that they were entitled under the Fifth Amendment to refuse to provide information to the Patuxent examiners. The court rejected the argument, however. It noted that the orders committing the defendants for examination provided that no information obtained could be used, either directly or indirectly, as a basis for subsequent criminal prosecution. Since the Fifth Amendment prohibits the compelling of testimony that may be used in future criminal cases, the appeals court held that the grant of immunity sufficiently protected the defendants' rights. The defendants also contended, however, that the Fifth Amendment privilege should protect them from the requirement of providing information that could be used to commit them as a defective delinquents. According to the court, "This contention turns on whether a defective delinquency proceeding is a criminal or a civil proceeding."[62] It cited the extensive authority for holding the proceedings to be civil, but added, "Of course, after Gault the mere attachment of the label of 'civil' to a proceeding does not resolve the question of whether the privilege against self-incrimination is applicable."[63] The court referred to a Maryland case that set up a test for juvenile proceedings:[64]

Under this two-pronged test a criminal case within the ambit of the Fifth Amendment is one where the State or Federal government seeks to impose a criminal or quasi-criminal sanction upon an individual for a violation of its law. In other words, a criminal case is one where the pertinent inquiry is into a violation of law and the consequence is a criminal or quasi-criminal sanction. . . .

A defective delinquency proceeding is not comparable to the provision in some states for a bifurcated trial where the jury first determines guilt or innocence and then, if the defendant is guilty, determines the sentence to be imposed, since under our statute an individual may not even be transferred to Patuxent for examination until after he has been convicted *and* sentenced [Emphasis in original] . . . .

A defective delinquency proceeding cannot be considered a "criminal case" within the ambit of the Fifth Amendment because it is not an inquiry into a violation of any law, but an inquiry into the mental and emotional status of an individual to ascertain whether that individual is a danger to society.[65]

The court found no denial of due process in the statute, and ruled that confining the two defendants under the contempt citation after the sentences expired did not violate their rights because the citation provided an independent basis for confinement. It suggested that their only option was to submit to the examinations, provide the information requested, and allow the Patuxent staff to make its diagnosis. If they were determined not to be defective delinquents, they would be released. "On the other hand, if after trial they are found to be defective delinquents, then for the protection of society they must be held under the provisions of the defective delinquency statute."[66]

A dissent to the opinion argued that the Fifth Amendment privilege ought to apply. The dissenters wrote:

If the possibility of a child's confinement in a juvenile institution until he reaches the age of twenty-one, based upon his being adjudicated "delinquent," is sufficient for the availability of the privilege against self-incrimination, then the danger of petitioners' confinement in a maximum security prison for possibly the rest of their lives, based upon their being criminally convicted and then being adjudicated "defective delinquents," is certainly sufficient for the availability of the privilege.[67]

A similar issue was considered in *McNeil* v. *Director, Patuxent Institution*, 407 U.S. 245 (1972): the petitioner raised the same Fifth Amendment issue as in *Williams*, but the court did not reach it. McNeil had also been held in Patuxent after the expiration of his sentence because he refused to cooperate in diagnostic interviews. At that time the state maintained that it had the authority to hold offenders until they cooperated and until the staff could conclude whether the offender was a defective delinquent. (See p. 79 for present provisions of the statute.) The court found it significant that the petitioner was being held on an *ex parte* order; the state maintained that since the commitment was only for observation, it did not need to be attended by such procedural safeguards as an adversary hearing. The court responded to this argument with the same reasoning it used in *Jackson* v. *Indiana*:[68] if a commitment may be permanent in effect, although based on a "temporary" order, it requires safeguards commensurate with long-term commitment; on the other hand, if the commitment is ordered with lesser safeguards on the grounds that it is temporary, then it must be effectively limited in length. The due process requirement is that the nature and length of the commitment must be rationally related to its purpose. Therefore, the court found, there must be some time limit on the length of a commitment for "observation." It did not set a specific limit, but suggested that the six months specified by statute for observation was a useful measure of the appropriate limit. It ruled that continuing to hold McNeil on the *ex parte* order a year after his five-year sentence had expired was a violation of due process.

The state had suggested that in view of the petitioner's recalcitrance, his continued confinement was analogous to civil contempt; the court responded that if contempt were the basis for the imprisonment, then a hearing was required to determine whether McNeil's behavior constituted contempt. "At such a hearing it could be ascertained whether petitioner's conduct is willful, or whether it is a manifestation of mental illness, for which he cannot fairly be held responsible."[69]

The state's third argument for the continued confinement was that McNeil was probably a defective delinquent because most noncooperators were. Therefore the confinement would rest not only on the need for observation, but also on the underlying purposes of the statute. The court said, "But that argument proves too much. For if the Patuxent staff members were prepared to conclude, on the basis of petitioner's silence and their observations of him over the years, that petitioner is a defective delinquent, then it is not true that he has prevented them from evaluating him. On that theory, they have long been ready to make their report to the court, and the hearing on defective delinquency could have gone forward."[70] McNeil was ordered released.

Justice William O. Douglas, in a concurring opinion, said that the privilege against self-incrimination ought to apply to McNeil. He noted that while in Patuxent McNeil was pursuing post-conviction remedies on his underlying conviction for assault, and that admissions to the Patuxent staff might have prejudiced his appeals.

The analogy between sexual psychopath proceedings and civil commitments has often been used to defend the sufficiency of procedural protections. As a result of a concerted movement in support of the rights of mental patients, however, the procedural standards for civil commitments have undergone some reconsideration in recent years. In a case with substantial implications for sexual psychopath statutes, *Lessard* v. *Schmidt*, [349 F. Supp. 1078 (E.D. Wis. 1972), vacated on other grounds, 414 U.S. 473 (1974)], a federal district court ruled that several procedural protections not usually offered in civil commitments were required under the Fourteenth Amendment's due process clause. They include the requirement of proof beyond a reasonable doubt and the privilege against self-incrimination. The court declined to rule that subjects of civil commitment proceedings are entitled to have counsel present during psychiatric examination, but it suggested that other means, such as recording interviews with psychiatrists, might be appropriate to ensure that counsel could effectively challenge expert testimony. It ruled that subjects of commitment proceedings were entitled to notice that they do not have to speak to psychiatrists, and notice that statements made to psychiatrists may be used to commit them. Further, a state cannot commit a person on the basis of statements to psychiatrists in absence of a showing that they were made with knowledge that the person was not required to speak.

This review of constitutional issues leaves unanswered many questions about what standards will be imposed in the future. It seems likely, however, that the basic approach of sexual psychopath statutes will continue to survive vagueness and equal protection challenges, that the distinction between civil and criminal proceedings will continue its slow decline in importance, and that continued litigation on specific procedural issues will result in requirements of more due process protection, as has been the case with juvenile proceedings.

Practical and Ethical Issues

Other objections to the sexual psychopath statutes remain. Since most of them apply to a wide range of criminal offenses, including nonviolent ones, and others concentrate exclusively on sex offenses, they are not particularly useful in singling out violent offenders for special handling. The volume of sexual psychopath litigation involving offenders charged with indecent exposure illustrates the fact that the statutes allow great expenditures of public resources for dealing with behavior that is not really a serious threat to public safety.

More serious than these problems is the fact that all the statutes involve confinement based on a prediction of criminal behavior. For reasons that will be discussed more fully in the concluding chapter, confinement based on predicted behavior rather than proven past behavior is not justified. The doubts expressed by the court in *Burnick* are substantial enough to establish that sexual psychopath and psychopathic offender laws are not an acceptable answer to problems of violent crime.

Notes

1. 221 A.2d at p. 406.

2. Code Ala. Tit. 15 § 434, Cal. Welfare & Institutions Code 6300 et seq., Colo. Rev. Stat. 16-13-201 et seq., Conn. Genn. Stat. Ann. 17-244 et seq., Fla. Stat. Ann. 917.13, Ga. Code Ann. 77-539, Smith-Hurd Ill. Ann. Stat. 38 § 105-1 to 105-2, Ind. Code 35-11-3.1-1 to 35-11-3.5-37, Iowa Code Ann. 225A.1 to 225A.15, Kan. Stat. Ann. 22-3429, Ann. Code Md. Art. 31B, Ann. Laws Mass. Chap. 123A, Minn. Stat. Ann. 526.09 et seq., Minn. Stat. Ann. 246.43, Vernon's Ann. Mo. Stat. 202.700 et seq., Rev. Stat. Neb. 29-2901 et seq., N.H. Rev. Stat. Ann. Chap. 173-A, N.J. Stat. Ann. 2A:164-3 to 2A:164-13, Ohio Rev. Code 2947.24 et seq., Ore. Rev. Stat. 426.510 et seq., Tenn. Code Ann. 33-1303, Utah Code Ann. 77-49-1, Vt. Stat. Ann. 18-8501, Rev. Code Wash. Ann. 71.06.010 et seq., Wis. Stat. Ann. 975.01 et seq., Wyo. Stat. 7-348 et seq., 22 D.C. Code 3501 et seq.

3. *Mass. Acts and Resolves*, Ch. 595, §§ 1-12 (1911).

4. Nicholas N. Kittrie, *The Right to be Different* (Baltimore: Penguin Books, 1971), p. 179. Reprinted by permission of Johns Hopkins University Press, Copyright © The Johns Hopkins Press, 1971.

5. Edwin H. Sutherland, "The Sexual Psychopath Laws," 40 *Journal of Criminal Law and Criminology* 543, 544 (1950). Reprinted by special permission of the Journal of Criminal Law and Criminology, Copyright © 1950 by *Northwestern University School of Law*, vol. 40, no. 5.

6. Ibid., p. 544.

7. Paul W. Tappan, "Some Myths About the Sex Offender," Federal Probation, Vol. 19, No. 2, p. 7 (1955).

8. Edwin H. Sutherland, "The Diffusion of Sexual Psychopath Laws," 56 *American Journal of Sociology* 142 (1950), reprinted in Richard Quinney, *Crime and Justice in Society* (Boston: Little, Brown and Company, 1969) pp. 88-97. Reprinted by permission of *American Journal of Sociology*. Copyright © 1950 by The University of Chicago.

9. Ibid., p. 89.

10. Ibid., p. 94.

11. Ibid., p. 93.

12. 309 U.S. at 273.

13. Kittrie, *The Right to Be Different*, pp. 170-171.

14. 295 F. Supp. at 398-399.

15. See Ohio Rev. Code 2907.05, 2907.06 (1975).

16. 295 F. Supp. at 414, 415.

17. 295 F. Supp. at 415.

18. 406 F.2d at 977, 978.

19. Alan M. Dershowitz, "Preventive Confinement: A Suggested Framework for Constitutional Analysis," 51 *Texas Law Review*, 1277, 1295 (1973). Reprinted by permission of Texas Law Review Publications, Inc.

20. Ibid., pp. 1295, 1296.

21. Ibid.

22. Ibid., pp. 1297, 1298.

23. Ibid., pp. 1298, 1299.

24. Ibid., pp. 1299, 1300.

25. See, e.g., *In re Gault*, 387 U.S. 1 (1966); *In re Winship*, 397 U.S. 358 (1970); *Lessard* v. *Schmidt*, 349 F. Supp. 1978 (E.D. Wis., 1972), vacated on other grounds, 414 U.S. 473 (1974).

26. See *Director* v. *Daniels*, 243 Md. 16, 221 A.2d 297, cert. den. 385 U.S. 940 (1966), quoted above, p. 42.

27. See, for example, *Millard* v. *Harris*, 406 F.2d 964 (D.C. Cir., 1968).

28. Alan A. Stone *Mental Health and Law: A System in Transition*, Rockville, Md.: Institute of Mental Health, Center for Studies of Crime and Delinquency, 1975, pp. 55-56.

29. *U.S. ex rel. Gerchman* v. *Maroney*, 355 F.2d 302 (3rd Cir., 1966), *Specht* v. *Patterson*, 386 U.S. 605 (1967).

30. 309 U.S. at 274-275.

31. 334 F.2d at 509.

32. 221 A.2d at 406-407.

33. 295 F. Supp. at 398.

34. 406 F.2d at 967.

35. *Durham* v. *U.S.*, 214 F.2d 862 (D.C. Cir., 1954).

36. 406 F.2d at 969.

37. 406 F.2d at 970.

38. 406 F.2d at 972.

39. 406 F.2d at 973.

40. 342 N.E.2d at 30.

41. Enacted Jan. 8, 1952, P.L. 1851, 19 Purdon's Pa. Stat. Ann. 1166-1174, no longer in effect.

42. 355 F.2d at 308, 309.

43. 355 F.2d at 309.

44. 381 U.S. 437.

45. 355 F.2d at 309.

46. 386 U.S. at 608, 609.

47. 334 F.2d at 512.

48. 344 F.2d at 513.

49. 221 A.2d at 410.

50. *Blizzard* v. *State*, 218 Md. 384, 147 A.2d 227 (1958).

51. 295 F. Supp. at 400.

52. 243 Md. 38-40, 221 A.2d 397.

53. 295 F. Supp. at 402.

54. 295 F. Supp. at 403.

55. 370 U.S. at 666-667.

56. 535 P.2d at 359.

57. 397 U.S. 358 (1970).

58. *Lessard* v. *Schmidt*, 349 F. Supp. 1078 (E.D. Wis., 1972), vacated on other grounds, 414 U.S. 473 (1974).

59. 535 P.2d at 364, 365.

60. 535 P.2d at 369.

61. 342 N.E.2d at 29, 520 F.2d at 937.

62. 347 A.2d at 191.

63. 347 A.2d at 194.

64. *Matter of Spalding*, 273 Md. 690, 332 A.2d 246 (1975).

65. 347 A.2d at 194, 195.

66. 347 A.2d at 201.

67. 247 A.2d at 203, 204.

68. 406 U.S. 715 (1972); see p. 111.

69. 407 U.S. at 251.

70. 407 U.S. at 251, 252.

3 Defendants Incompetent to Stand Trial

Statutes concerning incompetence to stand trial are relevant to our interests because they apply to mentally ill or mentally deficient persons charged with crimes. These people, of course, are frequently considered dangerous both by the public and by medical experts. Further, incompetence statutes have been used at times to incapacitate such defendants, often for long periods, without convicting them of crimes. It will be useful to consider these statutes in connection with the issues of mental illness and violence, prediction of violent behavior, and incapacitation of offenders who are considered dangerous.

Competence to stand trial has long been considered a necessary element of a fair criminal proceeding, since an effective defense requires the defendant's cooperation in providing his attorney with factual information and suggesting theories to establish his innocence. Under *Bishop* v. *United States,* 350 U.S. 961 (1956), competence is an element of due process.

Every state except Washington has a statute providing for the disposition of defendants found incompetent to stand trial.[1] Blackstone has described the historical reason for the rule:

In criminal cases, therefore, idiots and lunatics are not chargeable for their own acts, if committed when under these incapacities; no, not even for treason itself. Also, if a man in his sound mind commits an offence, and before arraignment for it he becomes mad, he ought not to be "called on to plead to it, because he is unable to do so" with that advice and caution that he ought. And if, after he has pleaded, the prisoner becomes mad, he shall not be tried; for how can he make his defence? If, after he be tried and found guilty, he loses his senses before judgement, judgment shall not be pronounced; and if, after judgment, he becomes of nonsane memory, execution shall be stayed, for peradventure, says the humanity of the English law, had the prisoner been of sound memory, he might have alleged something, in stay of judgment of execution. . . . For, as is observed by Sir Edward Coke, "the execution of an offender is for example, [that the punishment may reach a few, but the fear of it affect all] : but so it is not when a madman is executed; but should be a miserable spectacle, both against law, and of extreme inhumanity and cruelty, and can be no example to others."[2]

Incompetence is most frequently defined, either in statutes or case law, as a mentally impaired defendant's inability to understand the nature of the criminal proceedings or to cooperate with counsel in his own defense. This is not, in fact, a difficult burden to meet, even in the case of defendants who would be immediately diagnosed as mentally ill. The report of a competence research

105

project at Harvard Medical School states: "It should be noted that defendants with mental disability of a serious degree, including psychosis and moderate mental retardation, frequently are quite competent . . . ." The researchers concluded that mental disability relates to competence only if it is manifested by malfunctioning in one of the specific areas of understanding of criminal proceedings that they outlined.[3]

The incompetence question may be raised at any time during a criminal prosecution, and, in fact, *Pate* v. *Robinson*, 383 U.S. 375 (1966), requires the prosecutor, the defense attorney, and the court to request an inquiry into the defendant's mental state at any time it appears that he might be incompetent.

Most statutes dealing with incompetence provide for a psychiatric examination of the defendant, at the request of the prosecutor or the defendant, or ordered by the court on its own motion. After the court receives the medical report, it holds a hearing to determine whether the defendant is competent, and what should be done with him if he is found incompetent. In some states the statute requires the defendant to be committed to a mental hospital (or a hospital for the criminally insane) and to be kept there until he becomes competent. In other states the court has discretion to order incompetent defendants committed, referred for outpatient care, or released. Most of the statutes outline some procedure for determining when the defendant has become competent and for returning him for trial.

Incompetence statutes have posed great difficulty, largely because incompetence is frequently confused with other issues involving the mental state of defendants—the insanity defense, or mental illness indicating a need for treatment but not relevant to the criminal proceedings. These difficulties have several sources:

1. Statutes often fail to distinguish incompetence from other mental health issues. Some states include the insanity defense or other treatment issues in the same section with provisions for incompetent defendants. Other states define incompetence in terms of insanity at the time of trial; some even purport to define incompetence to be identical with insanity relieving the defendant of criminal responsibility. Some states do not define incompetence by statute; rather it is controlled by case law.
2. Courts often reveal confusion about mental health issues involving criminal defendants. If they do understand the distinctions, they may fail to make clear to examining psychiatrists or psychologists exactly what constitutes incompetence or to ask for a medical report in the form of answers to specific questions.
3. Mental health professionals demonstrate even more confusion over the terms "incompetent" and "insane." Their reports frequently employ medical language that is not very helpful to courts, and offer conclusions rather than specific information.

Statutory Definitions

Some states spell out in their statutes the usual definition of incompetence as described above. California defines a defendant as incompetent if he is "unable to understand the nature of the proceedings and assist counsel in the conduct of a defense in a rational manner." The New York statute refers to a person who, as a result of mental disease or defect, lacks capacity to understand the proceedings against him or to assist in his own defense. Others are less specific. North Carolina's statute applies to any defendant who "shall be found by the court to be without sufficient mental capacity to undertake his defense." The statutes of some states (e.g., Hawaii, New Jersey, Ohio, Oklahoma, and South Dakota) simply state that a defendant may not be tried if he is insane at the time of the proceeding.

Other states include in the same section more than one issue involving the defendant's mental state. The New Hampshire statute says, "in either of the aforementioned cases [incompetence to stand trial or acquittal by reason of insanity], the court if it is of the opinion that it will be dangerous that such person should go at large, may commit him to the prison or to the state hospital for life until or unless earlier discharged, released, or transferred by due course of law."[4] The section of the Utah statutes dealing with defendants who are incompetent to stand trial also includes those who become insane while serving prison terms. One section of the District of Columbia code applies to defendants who are either incompetent to stand trial or "of unsound mind." A few states (e.g., Arkansas, Iowa, Nevada, Texas, and Utah) purport to define incompetence to be the same as insanity.

Some incompetence statutes apply both to mentally ill and mentally deficient defendants; some do not make clear whether they apply to both groups.

Table 3-1 indicates whether the statute includes the most frequent definition of incompetence, whether it specifically mentions mental illness, mental deficiency or "insanity," and whether it provides a different definition of incompetence.

Considering this statutory confusion over the meaning of incompetence, it should not be surprising that the questions asked of psychiatrists who examine defendants often fail to provide useful guidance for their determination. As Alan Stone put it, "Since the court refers defendants [for examination] in an ambiguous manner and asks both legal questions [competence and criminal responsibility] at the same time, and since the insanity defense is more familiar, it is easy to understand how psychiatrists might become confused."[5]

Stone also pointed out: "Unfortunately few psychiatrists understand the distinction between competency and criminal responsibility. In fact, most psychiatrists equate psychosis with insane (not criminally responsible) and they assume insane includes incompetent to stand trial. In fact, the American

Table 3-1
Incompetence to Stand Trial

	Standard Definition	Specific Mention of Mental Illness	Specific Mention of Insanity	Specific Mention of Mental Defect	Other Definition of Incompetence
Alabama	No	No	Yes	No	Insanity of those charged, in confinement awaiting trial
Alaska	Yes	Yes	No	Yes	—
Arizona	Yes	Yes	No	Yes	—
Arkansas	No	No	Yes	No	Insanity, not knowing difference between right and wrong
California	Yes	No	No	No	—
Colorado	Yes	Yes	No	Yes	—
Connecticut	Yes	No	Yes	Yes	—
Delaware	Yes	Yes	No	Yes	—
Florida	No	No	Yes	No	Same as insanity
Georgia	Yes	No	No	No	—
Hawaii	No	No	Yes	No	Defendant is insane
Idaho	Yes	Yes	No	Yes	—
Illinois	Yes	No	No	No	—
Indiana	No	No	No	No	No definition
Iowa	No	No	Yes	No	Same as insanity
Kansas	Yes	No	No	No	—
Kentucky	Yes	No	No	No	—
Louisiana	Yes	Yes	No	Yes	—
Maine	No	Yes	No	Yes	"Competence to stand trial" mentioned but not defined
Maryland	Yes	No	No	No	—
Massachusetts	No	No	No	No	No definition
Michigan	Yes	No	No	No	—
Minnesota	Yes	No	No	No	—
Mississippi	No	No	Yes	Yes	Defendant was insane at time of offense and still is insane to such an extent as not to be responsible for act or omission
Missouri	Yes	No	No	No	—
Montana	Yes	No	No	No	—
Nebraska	No	No	No	No	Statute refers to incompetence to stand trial but doesn't define it
Nevada	No	No	No	No	Same as insanity

Table 3-1 (cont.)

	Standard Definition	Specific Mention of Mental Illness	Specific Mention of Insanity	Specific Mention of Mental Defect	Other Definition of Incompetence
New Hampshire	No	No	No	No	Statute refers to incompetence to stand trial but doesn't define it
New Jersey	No	No	Yes	No	Insanity at time of hearing
New Mexico	No	No	No	No	No definition
New York	Yes	Yes	No	Yes	–
North Carolina	No	No	No	No	No definition
North Dakota	Yes	Yes	No	Yes	–
Ohio	No	No	Yes	No	Insanity during criminal proceedings
Oklahoma	No	No	Yes	No	Present insanity (case notes indicate that test is standard definition)
Oregon	Yes	Yes	No	Yes	–
Pennsylvania	Yes	No	No	No	–
Rhode Island	Yes	No	No	No	–
South Carolina	Yes	No	No	No	–
South Dakota	No	Yes	No	No	Statute says only that a mentally ill person can't be tried
Tennessee	No	Yes	No	No	"Incompetent to stand trial because of mental illness"
Texas	No	No	Yes	No	Present insanity
Utah	No	No	Yes	No	Insanity
Vermont	No	No	No	No	No definition
Virginia	Yes	No	No	No	–
Washington[a]					
West Virginia	Yes	No	No	No	–
Wisconsin	Yes	Yes	No	Yes	–
Wyoming	Yes	Yes	No	Yes	–
Federal	Yes	No	Yes	No	–
District of Columbia	Yes	No	No	No	Incompetence defined in standard terms, but provisions of statute apply both to persons who are incompetent and those of "unsound mind"
Puerto Rico	No	No	No	No	No definition

[a]No statute.

Psychiatric Association's glossary perpetuates this error: 'Insanity: A vague legal term for psychosis, now obsolete in psychiatric usage. Generally connotes: (a) a mental incompetence, (b) inability to distinguish right from wrong, etc.' "[6]

This legal and psychiatric confusion over the meaning of incompetence has greatly limited the availability of legally useful evaluations of the mental states of defendants. The Harvard project report put it this way: "There is certainly nothing new in the observation that the disciplines of psychiatry and the law have had difficulty in communicating with each other . . . . Thus, when a court takes the trouble (which it usually doesn't) to articulate the tripartite common law criteria for competency and gets back the answer 'Schizophrenia,' we are witnessing the interdisciplinary lack of rational communication which has governed the handling of the competency issue in this country with rare exceptions."[7]

The report also suggested that psychiatrists may not be the only discipline or even the best discipline to determine the defendant's competence.

There appear to be four basic requirements for an examiner or "expert" on the issue of competency: (1) an adequate knowledge of the criminal justice system; (2) adequate interpersonal skills in interviewing and eliciting relevant, legally-oriented data from defendants who are mentally ill or mentally retarded; (3) knowledge and application of criteria for competency, and (4) professional status to assure credibility. Given these requirements, it is at once apparent that psychiatrists (and psychologists and social workers), unless they have had adequate criminal process experience, are likely to lack sufficient knowledge of the criminal justice system and knowledge and application of criteria for competence. Lawyers (with criminal bar experience) will be strong in the first but generally weak in the second. We would suggest that any of the three alternative professional groups mentioned (as well as others), with adequate training and experience in their weaker area, could do at least as satisfactory a job in competency proceedings as psychiatrists have up to now.[8]

Notwithstanding these difficulties with psychiatric information on competence, thirty-two of the statutes specifically require a medical or psychiatric examination if a question of competence is raised.[a] The statutes provide variously for the examination to be made by consulting physicians or psychiatrists or by the staff of a state mental institution.

In almost every jurisdiction, the decision on competence is made by the court. Ten states mention a right to jury trial. Four statutes do not specify who makes the determination; presumably it is the court.[b] The Oklahoma statute provides that the decision will be made by the state hospital staff.

[a]States that do not specifically require an examination are Alabama, Delaware, Florida, Georgia, Hawaii, Iowa, Kansas, Kentucky, Louisiana, Minnesota, Nebraska, New Hampshire, New Mexico, New York, North Carolina, Ohio, Pennsylvania, South Dakota, Texas, and the District of Columbia.

[b]Alabama, Arkansas, California, Georgia, Hawaii, Illinois, Iowa, Kansas, Ohio, and Texas mention a jury trial. Indiana, Kentucky, New Hampshire, and South Dakota do not specify who determines competence.

In twenty-eight states commitment to some kind of institution is required if the defendant is found to be incompetent. In one additional state, commitment is required if the defendant is found to be dangerous. In nineteen of the twenty-eight, the commitment apparently continues until the defendant regains competence. Table 3-2 shows whether the commitment is mandatory or discretionary for incompetent defendants, and whether the commitment continues until the defendant becomes competent.

The length of the commitment is important, because it has not been uncommon for defendants to be diverted from the criminal justice system to the mental health system for long periods through incompetence proceedings, or simply to be "lost" in a state hospital system for very long periods. According to Stone, "Data demonstrate that far more persons are confined on the basis of incompetence than because they have been found not guilty by reason of insanity. An incompetent defendant often could expect to spend his life in a hospital for the criminally insane. In 1972, 8,825 men, 5,349 of whom were nonwhite, were committed as incompetent" [citation omitted] .[9]

Most statutes provide for another court determination of competence when it appears that the defendant has become competent. A few leave the decision to the institutional staff; a few allow the defendant to petition for a new determination when he believes himself competent for trial; and a few require regular reports to the court on the condition of the defendant, or treatment plans directed toward restoring competence.

The Supreme Court considered the commitment of incompetent defendants in *Jackson* v. *Indiana*, 406 U.S. 715 (1972). The case involved a mentally deficient deaf-mute, who had been charged with two robberies, found to lack the capacity to understand the charges against him or to communicate with counsel or court officials, and committed by the trial court to the Indiana Department of Mental Health until it could certify him "sane." Examining physicians had testified that in their opinion the defendant was incapable of learning enough sign language to communicate with counsel and others concerning the criminal proceeding, and that even if he were able to communicate, he probably lacked the intellectual capacity to understand the charges against him or the import of court proceedings.

Jackson's counsel maintained that the state should have been required to commit him under the regular process for civil commitment of mentally ill or "feeble-minded" persons. The civil procedure involved a narrower definition of the conditions for which commitment was appropriate, provided for more adequate care and education during confinement, and offered a more lenient standard for release. If civilly committed, Jackson probably would have been eligible for release within a short time, since previously he had been able to hold a job and take care of himself with help from relatives.

The court ruled that institutionalizing Jackson under a standard that made it easier to commit him and more difficult for him to obtain release than would

Table 3-2
Commitment of Incompetent Defendants

State	Nature of Commitment	Length of Commitment
Alabama	Mandatory	Until competent
Alaska	Discretionary	Until competent
Arkansas	Discretionary	—
Arizona	Discretinary	—
California	Mandatory	—
Colorado	Mandatory	Until competent
Connecticut	Mandatory	—
Delaware	Discretionary	Until competent
Florida	Mandatory	—
Georgia	Mandatory	—
Hawaii	Mandatory	—
Idaho	Mandatory	Until competent
Illinois	Discretionary	—
Indiana	Discretionary	—
Iowa	Mandatory (if dangerous)	Until competent
Kansas	Discretionary	Until competent
Kentucky	Discretionary	—
Louisiana	Mandatory	Until competent
Maine	Mandatory	—
Maryland	Discretionary	—
Massachusetts	Referred to civil commitment	—
Michigan	Discretionary	—
Minnesota	Mandatory	Until competent
Mississippi	Mandatory	Until competent
Missouri	Mandatory	Until competent
Montana	Mandatory	Until competent
Nebraska	Mandatory	Until competent
New Hampshire	Discretionary	Until competent
New Jersey	Discretionary	—
New Mexico	Discretionary	—
New York	Mandatory	—
Nevada	Mandatory	Until competent
North Carolina	Mandatory	Until competent
North Dakota	Mandatory	—
Ohio	Mandatory	Until competent
Oklahoma	Mandatory	Until competent
Oregon	Discretionary	Until competent
Pennsylvania	Discretionary	Until competent
Rhode Island	Mandatory	—

Table 3-2 (cont.)

State	Nature of Commitment	Length of Commitment
South Carolina	Discretionary	–
South Dakota	Discretionary	Until competent
Tennessee	Discretionary	–
Texas	Discretionary	Until competent
Utah	Mandatory	Until competent
Vermont	Discretionary	Until competent
Virginia	Mandatory	Until competent
West Virginia	Mandatory	–
Wisconsin	Mandatory	Until competent
Wyoming	Mandatory	Until competent
Federal	Discretionary	Until competent
District of Columbia	Mandatory	Until competent
Puerto Rico	Discretionary	Until competent

have been the case for other involuntarily hospitalized persons constituted a denial of equal protection. Citing *Baxstrom* v. *Herold*, 383 U.S. 107 (1966), the court found the criminal charges filed against Jackson insufficient grounds for this different treatment. The court also held that committing Jackson indefinitely on the sole basis of his inability to stand trial was a denial of due process:

We hold, consequently, that a person charged by a State with a criminal offense who is committed solely on account of his incapacity to proceed to trial cannot be held more than the reasonable period of time necessary to determine whether there is substantial probability that he will attain that capacity in the foreseeable future. If it is determined that this is not the case, then the state must either institute the customary civil commitment proceeding that would be required to commit indefinitely any other citizen, or release the defendant. Furthermore, even if it is determined that the defendant probably soon will be able to stand trial, his continued commitment must be justified by progress toward that goal.[10]

This standard resolves itself into three separate requirements:

1. No defendant who is declared incompetent may be committed for longer than the period needed to determine whether there is a substantial probability that he will become competent in the foreseeable future.
2. Incompetent defendants who are not likely to become competent in the foreseeable future must be released or referred to civil commitment procedures.
3. Incompetent defendants who are expected to become competent in the

foreseeable future must be making progress toward competence to justify keeping them in a mental institution. This would require periodic reevaluations of their conditions and prognosis.

Clearly, statutes that provide for commitments of incompetent defendants until they regain competence are not by their terms in compliance with *Jackson*, although it is possible that defendants are actually dealt with in accordance with the decision. Statutes of several states (e.g., California, Illinois, Indiana, and North Dakota) appear to have been written in an attempt to comply with the *Jackson* requirements.

Table 3-3 shows whether there are provisions in each state's statute to meet the *Jackson* standard.

Usefulness

Two factors are of major importance in assessing the usefulness of incompetence statutes for incapacitating or treating violent offenders. The first of these is the narrowness of the definition of incompetence as properly distinguished from other mental health issues. The number of mentally ill defendants who are actually unable to understand the nature of the charges against them or to assist counsel in their own defense may be quite small, and the fact of incompetence does not seem to be related to the seriousness of the offense charged.

The second factor is the limitations placed on commitment of incompetent defendants by *Jackson* v. *Indiana.* Compliance with this constitutional standard means that defendants who are incompetent may be committed for short periods for evaluation and treatment, but if competence is not restored within a few months, they will be referred to the civil commitment procedures for a determination on the need for indeterminate hospitalization.

Consideration of these two factors indicates that incompetence statutes are of very little use either in distinguishing dangerous offenders from others or in incapacitating or treating them. Any use of such statutes for long-term restraint of dangerous offenders or for attempting to change their behavior would require substantial abuse of the definition of incompetence and of the constitutional standards presently outlined. In addition, since these persons have not been convicted of the offenses charged, we consider it clearly unethical and unacceptable to act on the assumption that they are guilty and that they should be restrained and treated under the guise of restoring them to capacity to stand trial. Although incompetence statutes may have served incapacitation and treatment functions in the past, they must be dismissed as neither appropriate nor effective means for dealing with the offenders who are the concern of this survey.

Notes

1. (Code Ala. Tit. 15, § 426, 428; Alas. Stat. 12.45.100; Ariz. R. Crim. P. 11.1; Ark. Stat. Ann., § 43-1301; Cal. Pen. Code 1367; Colo. Rev. Stat. 16-8-110

Table 3-3
Limitations on Commitments

State	Are commitments limited to the time needed to determine whether the defendant probably will become competent in the foreseeable future?	What provisions are made for defendants not likely to become competent in the foreseeable future?	Are periodic checks required to insure that continued commitment is justified by progress toward regaining competence?
Alabama	No	None	No
Alaska	No	None	No
Arizona	Yes	None	Court may require reports
Arkansas	Length not specified	None	No
California	Yes	Conservatorship proceedings	Yes
Colorado	No	No	No
Connecticut	No	None	No
Delaware	No	None	No
Florida	Not clear[a]	Verdict of not guilty by reason of insanity; referred for civil commitment proceedings	Yes
Georgia	No	None	No
Hawaii	No	None	No
Idaho	No	None	No
Illinois	Not clear[a]	Court may release incompetent defendants who no longer need hospitalization	No
Indiana	Yes	Civil commitment proceedings	Yes
Iowa	No	None	No
Kansas	No	Hospital may parole incompetent defendants if appropriate	No
Kentucky	Defendants thought to be incompetent referred for civil commitment proceedings.		
Louisiana	No	Court may order release if hospital superintendent finds it safe	No
Maine	No	Civil commitment proceedings	No
Maryland	No	Charges may be dismissed after five years	Hospital must make annual reports
Massachusetts	Not clear[a]	None specified; release may be possible	No
Michigan	No	Referral to civil commitment after 15 months or one-third of maximum sentence	None required after report on original examination
Minnesota	No	None	No

Table 3-3 (cont.)

State	Are commitments limited to the time needed to determine whether the defendant probably will become competent in the foreseeable future?	What provisions are made for defendants not likely to become competent in the foreseeable future?	Are periodic checks required to insure that continued commitment is justified by progress toward regaining competence?
Mississippi	No	None	No
Missouri	No	None	No
Montana	No	None	No
Nebraska	No	None	No
Nevada	No	None	No
New Hampshire	No	None	No
New Jersey	No	None	No
New Mexico	No	None	No
New York	Not clear[a]	Civil commitment proceedings required after two-thirds of maximum sentence	No
North Carolina	No	None	No
North Dakota	Yes	Charges dismissed; referral for civil commitment	Yes
Ohio	No	None	No
Oklahoma	No	None	No
Oregon	No	Court may dismiss charges and refer for civil commitment after unspecified period	No
Pennsylvania	No	None	No
Rhode Island	No	Court has discretion to terminate commitment	Annual report, including prognosis, required
South Carolina	Yes	Referred for civil commitment proceedings	Yes
South Dakota	No	None	No
Tennessee	Defendants in need of mental health care referred for civil commitment proceedings.		
Texas	No	None	No
Utah	No	None	No
Vermont	After commitment, incompetent defendants are governed by civil commitment statutes.		
Virginia	Defendants found incompetent referred for civil commitment proceedings.		
Washington	No statute.		
West Virginia	Yes	Charges dismissed; re ferred for civil commitment proceedings	No
Wisconsin	No	Court may dismiss charges and begin civil commit-	No

Table 3-3 (cont.)

State	Are commitments limited to the time needed to determine whether the defendant probably will become competent in the foreseeable future?	What provisions are made for defendants not likely to become competent in the foreseeable future?	Are periodic checks required to insure that continued commitment is justified by progress toward regaining competence?
		ment proceedings when maximum sentence has expired	
Wyoming	No	Referral for civil commitment	Reports required every three months
Federal	No	None	No
District of Columbia	No	None	No
Puerto Rico	No	None	No

aIndicates that the statute provides a time limit, but does not mention a determination of whether the defendant will be competent in the foreseeable future.

to 16-8-113; Conn. Gen. Stat. Ann. 54-50; Del. Code Ann. Tit. 11, § 404; Fla. R. Crim. P. 3.210(a); Ga. Code Ann. 27-1504; Hawaii Rev. Stat. 711-92; Idaho Code 18-212; Smith-Hurd Ill. Ann. Stat. Chap. 38, § 1005-2-1, 1005-2-2; Ind. Code 35-5-3.1-1 to 35-5-3.1-5; Iowa Code Ann. 783.1 to 783.4; Kan. Stat. Ann. 22-3301; Ky. Rev. Stat. Ann. 504.040; La. Code of Crim. P. 641; Me. Rev. Stat. Ann. Chap. 15, § 101; Ann. Code Md. Art. 59, §§ 23, 24, 28; Ann. Laws Mass. 123:15 to 123:17; Mich. Comp. Laws Ann. 330.2020; Minn. Stat. Ann. 611.026, 631.18; Miss. Code Ann. 99-13-3 to 99-13-5; Vernon's Ann. Mo. Stat. 552.020; Rev. Codes of Mont. 95-505; Nev. Rev. Stat. 178.425; N.H. Rev. Stat. Ann. 651.9; N.J. Stat. Ann. 2A:163-2; N.M. Stat. Ann. 41-13-3.1; McKinney's N.Y. Crim. P. Law 730.10 to 730.70; Gen Stat. N.C. 122-84; N.D. Century Code 12.1-04-04 to 12.1-04-09; Ohio Rev. Code 2945.37; Okla. Stat. Ann. Chap. 22, §§ 1171 to 1174; Ore. Rev. Stat. 161.360, 161.365, 161.370; Purdon's Pa. Stat. Ann. Chap. 50, §§ 4408, 4409; Gen. Laws R.I. 26-4-3; Code Laws S.C. 32-977; S.D. Comp. Laws 23-38-1 to 23-38-7; Tenn. Code Ann. 33-708; Vernon's Tex. Code Crim. P. 46.02; Utah Code Ann. 77-48-2 to 77-48-6; Vt. Stat. Ann. Tit. 13, §§ 4814 to 4822; Code Va. 19.2-167 to 19.2-169; W. Va. Code 27-6A-1, 27-6A-2; Wis. Stat. Ann. 971.13, 971.14; Wyo. Stat. 7-242.2; 18 U.S. Code 4244; 24 D.C. Code 301; Laws P.R. Ann. Tit. 34 R.240.)

2. William Blackstone, *Commentaries on the Laws of England: of Public Wrongs*, adapted by Robert Malcolm Kerr, (Boston: Beacon Press, 1962), pp. 21-22.

3. *Competency to Stand Trial and Mental Illness* Laboratory of Community Psychiatry, Harvard Medical School, National Institute of Mental Health, Center for Studies of Crime and Delinquency, Rockville, Md., p. 100. Hereafter cited as Harvard Report.

4. N.H. Rev. Stat. Ann. 651.9.

5. Alan A. Stone, *Mental Health and Law: A System in Transition* (Rockville, Md.: National Institute of Mental Health, Center for Studies of Crime and Delinquency, 1975), p. 203.

6. Ibid., pp. 202-203.

7. Harvard Report, p. 1.

8. Ibid., p. 64.

9. Stone, *Mental Health and Law*, p. 203.

10. 406 U.S. at 738.

4

Disposition After Acquittal By Reason of Insanity

Several mental health issues are again joined in the question of what should be done with a defendant who has been acquitted on grounds of insanity. Although these people have been found not criminally responsible for their acts because of their mental state at the time of the offense, the public often believes, and many state statutes presume, that they continue to pose a danger to society. Since laws providing for the institutionalization of such defendants are another possible way of incapacitating and treating persons considered dangerous, the various schemes for dealing with them will be described.

This survey is not concerned with the exact standard for acquittal on grounds of insanity. The debate over the M'Naghten rule, the *Durham* rule,[1] the irresistable impulse test, and other formulations has been carried on for many years by eminent legal minds, and this study need not enter into it. It is sufficient for present purposes that through some legal procedure a defendant has been found to be mentally disordered to such a degree that society believes it would be unjust or inappropriate to impose criminal responsibility for his acts. This chapter is concerned with what happens to the defendant after this determination has been made.

The first issue that arises is the question of the exact import of a verdict of not guilty by reason of insanity. Such a verdict indicates a finding by the jury or court that the defendant did the act charged; otherwise the verdict would have been simply "not guilty." It is more difficult to determine, however, any implication or presumption relating to the mental state or dangerousness of the defendant at the time of the verdict. One court concluded that under the reasonable doubt standard for conviction,

... such an acquittal means only that there was a reasonable doubt concerning the defendant's sanity [criminal responsibility] at the time he committed a prohibited act. It is possible that he was sufficiently sane to have criminal responsibility; indeed, under the applicable standard, it may be more likely than not.

Moreover, "meaningful elements of responsibility" may exist even in those cases in which the jury is certain that the defendant was not "sufficiently responsible." The insanity defense is not a matter of black and white—there is not a precise psychological line separating absolute free will from absolute uncontrollability. Rather, the defense is based on a balance between mental disease and self-control, the law having determined that a person should not be found guilty when the former is such that the latter becomes, not non-existent, but merely "substantially impaired" .... Even those defendants

119

who are "legally insane" to a "certainty," in other words, may have some control over their behavior, and therefore may possess some "meaningful elements of responsibility for the offense."[2,a]

It is therefore possible to say at minimum that any defendant acquitted on grounds of insanity is a person who has committed a criminal act, but who is not held responsible for it because of some degree of mental disease. Theoretically, one might argue that such a person poses an inherent danger, in that the lack of ability to control behavior that led to his acquittal might lead to the commission of further prohibited acts. The mental state involved, however, is that of the defendant at the time of the act charged, which may be months or even years in the past at the time of the acquittal. The implications for the future behavior of defendant, or for his need for further institutional treatment, seem difficult to pin down merely on the basis of a verdict of not guilty by reason of insanity.

In spite of these difficulties, many statutes dealing with disposition of such persons have carried the often unstated assumption that they pose a clear threat of further criminal behavior, and specifically of physical harm to other persons. The general presumption that a mental state continues once it is proved to exist, in absence of evidence of a change, adds force to the assumption behind these statutes.

Like incompetence statutes, these laws create substantial confusion because of their terminology. The word "insanity," in this context, usually refers to the lack of criminal responsibility discussed above. But the statutes refer to the defendant's "sanity" at the time of acquittal, and some of them refer to the restoration of "sanity" as a criterion for release. It is not clear from most of these statutory references whether the word "insanity" is being equated with mental illness. If such is the intent, the terminology seems poorly chosen; on the other hand, if "sanity" and "insanity" are used in the sense of criminal responsibility or lack of criminal responsibility, these terms would seem to have very little meaning with respect to the defendant's mental state after acquittal. Such terms as "restored to reason" seem similarly lacking in meaning.

The issue of disposition of defendants acquitted by reason of insanity has been considered of sufficient importance that every jurisdiction except Florida and the federal government has a statute dealing with the problem. (Federal defendants who are acquitted by reason of insanity are made available to state authorities for civil commitment proceedings. The proposed new federal criminal code as originally introduced in S. 1 includes provisions for the federal government to commit such defendants to federal mental institutions.)[3]

---

[a]This analysis is of acquittal under the *Durham* rule; if a defendant may be acquitted under this rule with a lesser degree of mental impairment than that required by the M'Naghten rule, then defendants acquitted under M'Naghten may be less responsible than this estimate would indicate.

General Approach of Statutes

Very few of the statutes concerned with the insanity defense require any finding in the verdict about the defendant's present mental state. The Mississippi statute does require that the verdict state whether the defendant has been restored to reason since the time of the offense, and whether he is dangerous to the community. The New Jersey statute also requires a finding on whether the defendant's insanity continues. The Oklahoma statute requires the verdict to state whether the defendant is presently dangerous to the public peace and whether he should be committed, but it does not appear to mandate a specific finding on his mental state at the time of acquittal. The Texas statute requires findings both on the defendant's present mental condition and on the question of whether he should be committed. The Ohio statute states that an acquittal on grounds of insanity creates a presumption that such insanity continues.

Some jurisdictions provide different dispositions for the defendant, depending on whether his insanity continues, or whether he has been restored to reason, but they do not specify how the mental state is to be determined. For example, California provides that the court must commit the defendant unless he appears to have recovered from his mental disorder. In that case he is to be referred for civil commitment proceedings.

The majority of jurisdictions do not require a new examination of the defendant to determine his present mental condition, but rather allow the decision on commitment to be made on the basis of psychiatric evidence presented in the trial. This evidence, of course, ordinarily is directed largely to the defendant's mental condition at the time of the offense. A few states give the trial court discretion to order another examination or not, and others specifically require one.

There are four basic approaches to disposition of defendants after acquittal. One is simply to begin civil commitment proceedings against them under the state's usual standards for involuntary hospitalization of mentally ill persons. Twelve states take th.s approach; in five, the civil commitment proceedings are required, and in the other seven the trial court has discretion to institute such proceedings or to release the defendant.

A second approach is to leave the decision on institutionalization to the trial court. This method is adopted in twenty states. The statutes provide varying degrees of guidance for the trial courts. In some states it is clear that the court must make a detailed new inquiry into the defendant's mental state, with a new examination, and a hearing on the issue of commitment. Other statutes seem to leave the question of commitment to the court's discretion, without requiring any new proceedings. Between these two extremes fall statutes that appear to contemplate some formal inquiry, rather than an order issued in the discretion of the court, but the statutes do not indicate what form the inquiry must take.

Eight jurisdictions require a temporary commitment after acquittal, to be followed by a court decision on whether the defendant should be released or should be committed for a longer period. In some of these states, this temporary commitment is treated much like a commitment for examination in a civil commitment or sexual psychopath proceeding, and the final commitment can be ordered only after a hearing at which the state has the burden of proving that the defendant falls within the class of persons for whom commitment is appropriate. In others, the temporary commitment becomes final unless the defendant requests a hearing and meets the burden of proof of his eligibility for release.

In fourteen states the trial court is required to order a final commitment of any defendant acquitted by reason of insanity.

There is some overlap among these four approaches. California, Louisiana, Mississippi, New Jersey, and Oklahoma provide different dispositions depending on the nature of the offense charged, on an informal assessment of the defendant's mental state, or on specific findings in the verdict. New Mexico and North Carolina require the trial court to conduct an inquiry on the issue of commitment using the state's civil commitment procedures. Indiana provides for the trial court inquiry followed by referral for civil commitment proceedings if the defendant is found to be mentally incompetent.

Table 4-1 shows the approach to institutionalization taken by each jurisdiction.

Commitments are indeterminate in almost every state, regardless of the procedure. In Connecticut and Wisconsin, commitments are limited to the maximum sentence that could be imposed for the offense charged. Georgia and Illinois limit commitments to one year; and Rhode Island, which provides for indeterminate commitments, requires annual review; Oregon limits commitments to five years; and Alabama, New Mexico, and Pennsylvania offer no indication of the length of commitments. Every other state provides for indeterminate commitments. (The length of commitments in states that employ civil commitment procedures has not been researched, since there is no special handling for the patients concerned in this chapter.)

Standards for Commitment and Release

In states that do not require commitment upon acquittal, the standards for commitment generally are similar to language used in civil commitment statutes. Many of them are drafted in terms of mental illness causing a danger to the public; however, some require commitment if the defendant has not recovered his "sanity." As noted above, this terminology seems to offer very little guidance for decision-makers.

The standards for release also are similar in many cases to those for civilly committed patients, allowing discharge when the patient is no longer mentally ill or no longer dangerous to himself or to others. The term "sanity" is occasionally used in this context also. In states that require a commitment upon acquittal but

Table 4-1
Each Jurisdiction's Approach to Institutionalization

Referral to Civil Commitment	Decision by Trial Court
Required	
Michigan	Alabama
Nebraska	Alaska
New Mexico (trial court inquiry under civil commitment standard)	Connecticut
	Hawaii
	Illinois
North Carolina (trial court inquiry under civil commitment standard)	Indiana
	Iowa
North Dakota	Louisiana (noncapital cases)
	Maryland
Discretionary	New Hampshire
Arizona	New Mexico (trial court inquiry under civil commitment standard)
Kentucky	
Massachusetts	North Carolina (trial court inquiry under civil commitment standard)
Pennsylvania	
South Carolina	Oregon
Tennessee	South Dakota
West Virginia	Texas
	Utah
	Vermont
	Washington
	Wyoming
	Puerto Rico

Temporary Commitment Required	Final Commitment Required
Arkansas	California (referral to civil commitment if defendant appears to have recovered)
Mississippi[a]	
Montana	Colorado
New York	Delaware
Rhode Island	Georgia
Virginia	Idaho
Wisconsin	Kansas
District of Columbia	Louisiana (capital cases)
	Maine
	Minnesota
	Missouri
	Nevada
	New Jersey[a]
	Ohio
	Oklahoma[a]

[a]Commitment is required only if the verdict says that the defendant is still insane or is dangerous.

provide for release when the defendant is no longer dangerous or no longer mentally ill, it would seem possible for some defendants to qualify for release immediately upon their admission to an institution. But in only four states are institution directors authorized to release patients without further court action. This may relieve some of the inconsistency in practice by requiring the patient to remain in the institution for a few weeks or months until a court can be persuaded that he should be released and until the formal processes are completed. The statutes, however, remain somewhat inconsistent on this point.

Table 4-2 shows standards for commitment and release (not including states that use civil commitment standards).

Usefulness and Constitutionality

It is obvious that the usefulness of these insanity defense statutes is limited with respect to dangerous offenders. Although such statutes probably would never be used to institutionalize offenders who had committed minor crimes, the total number of offenders who will be affected by the statutes is very small.

The major constitutional cases concerning commitment after acquittal by reason of insanity arose under a statute that was passed in the District of Columbia after the *Durham* decision and that required commitment upon such acquittal. *Ragsdale* v. *Overholser*, 281 F.2d 943 (D.C. Cir. 1960), dealt with the standard for release from involuntary commitment following acquittal. The patient in this case was charged with robbery and, after acquittal, committed to St. Elizabeths Hospital. He had left the hospital without leave and had spent ten months working, apparently without symptoms of mental illness, before being taken into custody again. He sought release on a writ of habeas corpus; under the standard then in effect, such a patient was required to prove beyond a reasonable doubt that he was not dangerous to himself or others in order to obtain release. The appeal court upheld this burden of proof, concluding that the statute applied to an exceptional class of people, and that its protective and rehabilitative purposes required both indeterminate commitments, which might last longer than the maximum term for the offense, and the burden of proof beyond a reasonable doubt. The court held that "reasonable medical doubts or reasonable judicial doubts are to be resolved in favor of the public and in favor of the subject's safety."[4] The order dismissing the patient's petition for a writ of habeas corpus was upheld.

Two years later, the Supreme Court considered the same statute in *Lynch* v. *Overholser*, 369 U.S. 705 (1962). In this case a defendant charged with passing two 50-dollar bad checks was referred to District of Columbia General Hospital to determine his competence to stand trial. The hospital's report stated that he was of unsound mind and was unable to understand the charges against him or to assist in his own defense. A later report said that Lynch had recovered

Table 4-2
Standards for Commitment and Release

State	Standard for Commitment	Standard for Release
Alabama	Insanity in any degree continues	Not specified
Alaska	Defendant is dangerous to public peace and safety	Disease is cured or defect corrected
Arkansas	Not specified	Patient has regained sanity
California	Commitment required	Sanity has been restored
Colorado	Commitment required	Patient no longer suffers from mental disease or defect making him dangerous to himself or others
Connecticut	Release would constitute danger to defendant or others	Patient is no longer so mentally ill as to be dangerous
Delaware	Commitment required	Public safety will not be endangered by release
Georgia	Commitment required	Patient no longer requires hospitalization
Hawaii	Insanity continues at time of acquittal	Insanity has ended
Idaho	Commitment required	Patient is not dangerous to himself or others
Illinois	Defendant is still insane	Patient is no longer in need of hospitalization
Iowa	Not specified	Patient is restored to good mental health and is no longer dangerous to himself or to the public peace
Kansas	Commitment required	Patient is not dangerous to himself or others
Louisiana	Release would cause danger to defendant or others	Release will not pose danger to patient or others
Maine	Commitment required	Patient will not endanger public peace and safety because of mental disease
Minnesota	Commitment required	Patient has improved sufficiently for release, and no person will be endangered by discharge
Mississippi	Defendant suffers from nervous or mental disorder and is in need of treatment, supervision or control, or is, or is likely to become, dangerous	Patient has been restored to reason
Missouri	Commitment required	Patient does not have, and in the reasonable future is not likely to have, mental disease or defect rendering him dangerous to safety of himself or others or unable to conform his conduct to the requirements of law
Montana	Release will cause danger to others	Patient may be released without danger to self or others

Table 4-2 (cont.)

State	Standard for Commitment	Standard for Release
Nevada	Commitment required	Patient has recovered
New Hampshire	Defendant is dangerous	Not specified
New Jersey	Defendant's insanity continues	Patient has been restored to reason
New Mexico	Defendant is mentally ill and likely to injure himself or others, or is in need of care, custody, or treatment	Not specified
New York	Defendant is dangerous to himself or others	Patient is no longer dangerous
Ohio	Commitment required	Patient's sanity has been restored, and release will not be dangerous
Oklahoma	Commitment required if verdict says defendant is dangerous to public peace	Not specified
Oregon	Defendant is still affected by mental disease or defect and presents a danger to himself or others, and is not a proper subject for release on supervision	Patient no longer poses substantial danger to himself or others
Rhode Island	Defendant suffers from mental disease or disorder to such an extent as to imperil the peace or safety of the people or himself	Patient is no longer dangerous
South Dakota	Release would be dangerous	Patient has become sane
Texas	Defendant is manifestly dangerous to public peace and safety	Patient has become sane
Utah	Defendant has not fully recovered his sanity	Patient's sanity has been restored
Vermont	Defendant is mentally ill and dangerous to himself and others or mentally ill and without sufficient capacity to make a responsible decision on care	Civil commitment standard for release applies
Virginia	Defendant is insane or feeble-minded and dangerous to himself or to the public peace and safety	Patient is no longer insane or feeble minded and no longer dangerous to himself or to the public peace and safety
Washington	Defendant poses substantial danger to himself or others and is in need of control by the court or other persons or institutions	There is no substantial likelihood of felonious acts jeopardizing public safety or security
Wisconsin	Defendant is still in need of care and treatment or is dangerous to himself and others	Patient is no longer in need of care and treatment or no longer a danger to himself or others

Table 4-2 (cont.)

State	Standard for Commitment	Standard for Release
Wyoming	Defendant is mentally ill and poses substantial risk of danger to himself or others and is not a proper subject for release on supervision	Patient is no longer affected by mental illness or deficiency, and is no longer dangerous to himself or others
District of Columbia	Not specified	Patient has recovered sanity and will not in the reasonable future be dangerous to himself or others
Puerto Rico	Defendant is mentally incompetent	Patient has become sane

competence to stand trial, but that he was a manic depressive, and that his disease would be likely to produce more crime. The report advised further treatment.

At the trial, Lynch attempted to change his plea from not guilty to guilty, but the court refused to accept the guilty plea. Expert witnesses for the prosecution testified, over the defendant's objections, that his crime had been committed as a result of mental illness; the defendant made no allegation of insanity or lack of responsibility. The court acquitted Lynch on grounds of insanity and ordered him committed to St. Elizabeths Hospital under the terms of the statute. Lynch maintained on appeal that applying the statute to defendants who claimed that their crimes were not the product of mental illness constituted a denial of due process. The court, in an opinion by Justice John M. Harlan, did not reach the constitutional issue, but ruled instead, as a matter of statutory construction, that the law in question was applicable only to defendants who had affirmatively relied on the insanity defense. The court found this result to be more consistent with the overall scheme of District of Columbia statutes concerning care of the mentally ill than was the government's position.

Cameron v. *Mullen*, 387 F.2d 193 (D.C. Cir., 1967), involved another defendant who had been found not guilty by reason of insanity, but who had not raised the defense herself. The charge in this case was misdemeanor assault, and the acquittal followed a psychiatric report indicating that the defendant was competent to stand trial but that she suffered from a "personality disturbance." She was committed to St. Elizabeths Hospital under the statute providing for commitment before sentencing of persons of unsound mind or those incompetent to stand trial. This statute had been used to commit persons acquitted on grounds of insanity following the ruling in *Lynch.* Cameron petitioned for release on habeas corpus, arguing that the statute had been improperly used to commit her. The court agreed, ruling that the purpose and form of the statute in question indicated that it was not intended for post-verdict commitments. The court also ruled that any suggestion in *Lynch* that this statute might be used for the same purpose was dictum. The court reviewed *Baxstrom* v. *Herold*, 383 U.S. 107 (1966), noting that *Baxstrom* stood for the principle that dangerousness is not relevant to procedures for determining whether a person is mentally ill, although it may be relevant to hospital security measures imposed on persons who have been shown by the usual procedures to be mentally ill.

"*Baxstrom* might also be said to require the conclusion that, while prior criminal conduct is a relevant consideration for determining the conditions of custodial care, it does not provide an automatic basis for allowing significant and arbitrary differences in such conditions."[5] Although the government maintained that Cameron had received all the benefits of a civil commitment proceeding, the court found several elements missing; she was not advised of her right to a de novo jury determination, and there had been no consideration of less restrictive measures, as would have been required for civil commitment. She was ordered released.

In *Bolton* v. *Harris*, 395 F.2d 642 (D.C. Cir. 1968), the court went further to extend the same protections to defendants who had affirmatively raised the defense of insanity. The court noted that the 1964 Hospitalization of the Mentally Ill Act required a judicial determination for civil commitments and placed the burden of proving mental illness on the government. The act also required the hospital to examine civilly committed patients at least every six months and to release them without the requirement of a court order if the chief of service considered them recovered.

The opinion said:

... in view of *Baxstrom* and the 1964 Act prior criminal conduct cannot be deemed a sufficient justification for substantial differences in the procedures and requirements for commitment.... The plea [of insanity] is neither an express nor implied admission of present illness, and acquittal rests only on a reasonable doubt of *past* sanity, i.e. at the time of the offense. It follows that there is no reasonable basis for distinction for commitment purposes between those who plead insanity and those who have the defense thrust upon them. Neither may be automatically deprived of the type of protection which the 1964 Hospitalization of the Mentally Ill Act provides.[6]

The opinion found, however, that it was constitutional to treat persons acquitted by reason of insanity differently from civilly committed patients "to the extent that there are relevant differences between these two groups."[7] According to the court, these relevant differences are sufficient to justify commitment without a hearing only for the time required to determine the defendant's mental condition. Any further period of commitment could be justified only by a judicial hearing with procedures substantially similar to civil commitments.

The court also upheld the release procedures provided in the statute for acquitted persons, which involved a hearing and made release more difficult than it would be for ordinary civilly committed patients. "We do not think equal protection is offended by allowing the Government or the court the opportunity to insure that the standards for the release of civilly committed patients are faithfully applied to [acquitted patients]."[8] The court concluded, "These modifications in no way alter the rule which the public safety has always required, namely, that persons who are dangerous due to mental illness be confined."[9]

The court considered release procedures in greater detail in *Waite* v. *Jacobs*, 475 F.2d 392 (D.C. Cir., 1973), and suggested that after the maximum sentence that could have been imposed had expired, equal protection required that the patient be given the same procedural benefits as civilly committed patients.

It seems to us that, after the expiration of the period for which an acquittee might have been incarcerated had he been convicted, it may be irrational, within the meaning of equal protection doctrine, to distinguish between an acquittee and a committee [civilly committed patient]. Acquittees who have been confined for that period, therefore, may be entitled to treatment no different from that afforded committees. Such a constitutional entitlement would necessitate that appellant be given a hearing at which the Government, in order to justify his continued confinement, would have to bear the burden of proof on the issues of mental illness and dangerousness.[10]

Because of difficulties in determining the precise basis of Waite's commitment, the court remanded the case for further consideration.

More recently, the District of Columbia Circuit Court has again upheld a higher standard for release for acquitted patients than for civilly committed ones, in *U.S.* v. *Ecker*, 543 F.2d 178 (D.C. Cir., 1976). The patient in this case was charged with rape and murder and was acquitted in 1968. This patient then would not fall into the *Waite* category in which the maximum possible sentence had expired. Emphasizing that the patient had committed violent crimes little more than two years after release from another mental hospital, the court found that the acquittal by reason of insanity did provide a rational basis for treatment different from other involuntary patients.

Conclusions

Statutes providing for disposition of defendants acquitted on grounds of insanity have attempted to deal with three problems: public fears of such defendants, reluctance to allow even mentally ill offenders to escape punishment, and the question of what kind of care or custody acquitted persons need. These statutes do apply to some of the violent offenders who are the concern of this study, but the number affected is probably very small. Many of the statutes do not offer a logical solution to the questions they are intended to address. As a group, they add little that is useful to the law concerning violent offenders.

Notes

1. *Durham* v. *U.S.*, 214 F.2d 862 (D.C. Cir., 1954).

2. *Waite* v. *Jacobs*, 475 F.2d 392, 396 (D.C. Cir., 1973).

3. Code Ala. Tit. 15, §§ 422-429; Alas. Stat. 12.45.090; Ark. Stat. Ann. 43-2135, 43-1301, 59-411; Ariz. R. Crim. P. 25; Cal. Pen. Code 1026; Colo. Rev. Stat. 16-8-105; Conn. Gen. Stat. Ann. 53a-47; Del. Code Ann. Tit. 11, § 403; Ga. Code Ann. 27-1503; Hawaii Rev. Stat. 711.92, 711.93; Idaho Code 18-213, 18-214; Smith-Hurd Ill. Ann. Stat. Chap. 38, §§ 115-3, 1005-2, 1005-4; Ind. Code 35-5-3.2-1; Iowa Code Ann. 785.19, Kan. Stat. Ann. 22-3428; Ky. Rev. Stat. Ann. 504.030; La. Code Crim. P. 654; Me. Rev. Stat. Ann. Chap. 15, §§ 103, 104; Ann. Code Md. Art. 59, §§ 23 to 28; Ann. Laws Mass. 123:16, 123:17; Mich. Comp. Laws Ann. 330.2050; Minn. Stat. Ann. 631.19; Miss. Code Ann. 99-13-7, 99-13-9; Vernon's Ann. Mo. Stat. 552.030, 552.040; Rev. Codes Mont. 95-505, 95-508; Rev. Stat. Neb. 29-2203; Nev. Rev. Stat. 178.425; N.H. Rev. Stat. Ann. 651:9; N.J. Stat. Ann. 2A:163-3; N.M. Stat. Ann. 41-23-25; McKinney's N.Y. Crim. P. Law 330.10; Gen. Stat. N.C. 122-84; N.D. Century Code 12.1-04-10; Ohio Rev. Code 2945.39; Okla. Stat. Ann. Chap. 22, §§ 925, 1161; Ore. Rev. Stat. 161.319 to 161.350; Purdon's Pa. Stat. Ann. Chap. 50, § 4413; Gen. Laws R.I. 26-4-4; Code Laws of S.C. 32-980; S.D. Comp. Laws 23-45-21; Tenn. Code Ann. 33-709; Vernon's Tex. Code Crim. P. 46.02; Utah Code Ann. 77-24-15, 77-24-16; Vt. Stat. Ann. Tit. 13, §§ 4819 to 4822; Code Va. 19.2-181, 19.2-182; Rev. Code Wash. Ann. 10:77.010, 10:77.090; W. Va. Code 27-6A-3, 27-6A-4; Wis. Stat. Ann. 971.17; Wyo. Stat. 7-246.6; 24 D.C. Code 301; Laws P.R. Ann. Tit. 34 R.241.

4. 281 F.2d at 947.

5. 387 F.2d at 201.

6. 395 F.2d at 649.

7. Ibid., at 651.

8. Ibid., at 652.

9. Ibid., at 653.

10. 475 F.2d at 395-396.

5

Hospitalization of Prison Inmates

This chapter is concerned with yet another issue involving the association between mental illness and violence: how to deal with prison inmates who need mental treatment. Because of their mental problems, these prisoners are often considered especially dangerous. The mentally ill prisoner has been thought to pose such serious problems of control and treatment that New York established mental hospitals as part of the corrections systems, and other states confine them in hospitals for the "criminally insane." This survey discovered forty-four statutes providing for hospitalization of mentally ill prisoners.[1,a]

Courts that have considered the transfer of prisoners to mental hospitals have discussed three separate kinds of legal injuries that can result from the transfer. The first is mental and emotional injury that can proceed from being mistakenly labeled as mentally ill and confined with mentally ill persons. The second is that the regimentation and loss of privacy and self-determination may be even greater in mental hospitals than in prisons. The third is possible prejudice to the inmate's parole rights, since some states do not permit parole consideration for hospitalized prisoners, and others may neglect to provide parole hearings for them.

The most important safeguard that courts have considered is the provision of a judicial hearing on the issue of mental illness before the prisoner is hospitalized. They have also considered the length of the mental hospital commitment, and whether it can have the effect of extending the prisoner's incarceration. Because the courts have given attention to these issues, this study will consider how the statutes treat them.

Perhaps the simplest approach, used in twelve states, is to hospitalize prison inmates under the state's civil commitment procedures.

A second approach to hospitalization of prison inmates is administrative transfer from the prison to a state mental hospital. Twenty-five jurisdictions have this type of statute.

A third approach requires a court order for hospitalization; these seven statutes provide varying degrees of court involvement. Some seem to be similar to civil commitment proceedings, requiring an examination and a hearing before the commitment order may be issued. Others appear to require a court inquiry, but they do not specifically mention an examination or hearing.

---

a A Tennessee statute authorizes civil commitment proceedings for prisoners who appear to be mentally ill and dangerous at the end of their sentences (Tenn. Code Ann. 41-348). There are no other provisions for hospitalization of prisoners.

Few of the statutes provide more than the bare outline of procedure, regardless of the approach taken. Typically, the administrative transfer statutes indicate little more than which official has the authority to order the transfer. For example, the Washington statute authorizes administrative transfer "[w]hen, in the judgment of the secretary of the department of social and health services, the welfare of any person committed to or confined in any state correctional institution or facility necessitates that such person be transferred or moved for observation, diagnosis or treatment to any state institution or facility for the care of the mentally ill."

Several statutes specifically require a psychiatric examination before such transfer; Hawaii requires a psychiatrist's certificate stating that the prisoner needs treatment. The federal statute establishes a board of examiners for each correctional institution, consisting of three medical officers, one of whom is a "competent expert in mental diseases." The board is to examine and report on any inmate "alleged to be insane or of unsound mind or otherwise defective." The attorney general is authorized to order the inmate transferred to a mental institution upon receipt of a report from the board of examiners.

Statutes requiring court action are not much more detailed. The Virginia statute says: "If any person, after conviction and sentencing for any crime, and while serving such sentence in any penal institution is declared by a commission of insanity to be insane or feebleminded, he shall be committed by the court to the proper hospital, and there kept until restored to sanity, and the time such person is confined in the proper hospital shall be deducted from the term for which he was sentenced."

Four states (Arizona, Illinois, Indiana, and Michigan) permit administrative transfer if the inmate consents; otherwise a court proceeding is required. This would seem to be the most efficient method since it eliminates the need for court involvement with consenting inmates, placing them in a situation similar to voluntary patients, while at the same time protecting the rights of inmates who do not want to be hospitalized.

As is clear from the above quotations, the statutes do not address the prisoner's rights or status while hospitalized. In most states the prisoner would be placed in a hospital for the criminally insane or in a secure ward of a state hospital.

Whether accomplished by administrative action or by court order, the transfer usually depends on the willingness of state hospital authorities to admit and treat the inmates. The Texas statute, for example, reads as follows: "The Director of the Department of Corrections may transfer a prisoner not under the death sentence who is confined in an institution operated by the Department of Corrections to a state mental hospital (or federal hospital), if a prison physician is of the opinion that he is mentally ill and would benefit from treatment in a mental hospital and if he is advised by the head of the hospital that facilities are available and the prisoner is eligible for treatment." Under most of the statutes, a state hospital decision that a prisoner was no longer in need of hospitalization would seem to require prison officials to transfer him back to a penal institution.

Not all the statutes specify what happens to the hospitalized prisoner when his prison term expires. If there is a civil commitment or other court proceeding before hospitalization, a separate judicial authority exists for confining the inmates after the prison sentence has expired. An inmate who had been administratively transferred into a hospital and kept there until his sentence expired would seem to be entitled to release unless civil commitment proceedings were instituted.

Even in states where the hospitalization of a prison inmate is limited by statute to the length of the sentence imposed, it is likely that hospitalized prisoners may spend much longer periods in penal custody than otherwise. Since most prison sentences imposed include a maximum term set by the court and since few prisoners serve their maximum sentences, a prisoner who is hospitalized until this maximum expires has in fact served a much longer time than if he had not been placed in a mental hospital.

A number of states require judicial commitment proceedings upon expiration of the prison sentence; some states require such proceedings even though the inmate has had a court hearing before being hospitalized. Although several states that allow administrative transfer do not specifically limit the hospitalization to the length of the sentence, none suggests that the inmate could be confined after his term had expired.

Prisoners who are hospitalized are not eligible for parole in some states; even if they are eligible, they may not be scheduled for parole hearings unless special care is taken to include them. The Washington statute is unusual in providing that "the secretary and the board of prison terms and paroles shall adopt and implement procedures to assure that persons so transferred shall, while detained or confined at such institute or facility for the care of the mentally ill, be provided with substantially similar opportunities for parole or early release evaluation and determination as persons detained or confined in the state correctional institutions or facilities."

Table 5-1 shows the procedure for hospitalizing a prisoner in each state that has a statute, and also lists the procedures required at the end of the prisoner's sentence. A few states have provisions for transferring prisoners to hospitals operated by the corrections department, or have both administrative and judicial hospitalization statutes. These statutes are summarized at the end of the table.

Federal courts considered the issue of transfer of prisoners into mental hospitals in two 1969 cases. The first was *U.S. ex rel. Schuster* v. *Herold*, 410 F.2d 1071 (2d Cir., 1969), cert. den., 396 U.S. 847 (1969). The prisoner involved had killed his wife and wounded her lawyer after a long and acrimonious divorce proceeding; his defense was that he acted in a "panic" and was not aware of what he was doing. The state's expert witnesses testified that he suffered from no mental disease. He was sentenced to a term of twenty-five

Table 5-1
Hospitalization of Mentally Ill Prison Inmates

State	Approach to Hospitalization	Procedure at End of Prison Term
Arkansas	Administrative transfer	Not specified
Arizona	Civil commitment; administrative transfer allowed if prisoner consents	Prisoner is discharged from prison confinement at end of sentence, but may be kept in hospital under commitment order
California	Administrative transfer	Not specified
Colorado	Administrative transfer	Not specified
Connecticut	Administrative transfer	New commitment proceeding required at end of prison sentence
Delaware	Court proceeding	Not specified
Florida	Administrative transfer	Commitment may not extend past end of sentence
Georgia	Administrative transfer	Inmate may petition for court determination of mental illness at end of sentence
Hawaii	Administrative transfer	Commitment limited to length of prison term
Illinois	Civil commitment; administrative transfer allowed if prisoner consents	New commitment proceeding required at end of sentence
Indiana	Administrative transfer, subject to inmate's right to court hearing on request	New commitment proceeding required at end of sentence
Iowa	Civil commitment	Not specified
Kansas	Administrative transfer	Civil commitment proceedings required at end of sentence
Kentucky	Administrative transfer	Civil commitment proceedings required at end of sentence
Louisiana	Court proceeding	Not specified
Maine	Inmate is referred to civil commitment procedures relating to emergency hospitalization	Not specified
Maryland	Civil commitment	Not specified
Massachusetts	Civil commitment	Not specified
Michigan	Administrative hearing; inmate is entitled to civil commitment proceedings on request	Not specified
Minnesota	Court proceeding	Not specified
Missouri	Administrative transfer	Commitment proceedings required at end of sentence
Nebraska	Administrative transfer	Not specified
Nevada	Civil commitment	Not specified
New Hampshire	Administrative transfer	Not specified

Table 5-1 (cont.)

State	Approach to Hospitalization	Procedure at End of Prison Term
New Jersey	Court proceeding	Commitment apparently can continue past end of prison sentence
North Carolina	Civil commitment	Commitment may extend past end of prison sentence
North Dakota	Administrative transfer	Not specified
Ohio	Administrative transfer	Court proceeding required at end of prison term
Oklahoma	Administrative transfer	Civil commitment proceedings required at end of sentence
Rhode Island	Court proceeding	Not specified
South Carolina	Civil commitment	Not specified
South Dakota	Administrative transfer	Not specified
Texas	Administrative transfer	Not specified
Utah	Court proceeding	Not specified
Vermont	Civil commitment	New commitment proceedings required at end of sentence
Virginia	Civil commitment	Not specified
Washington	Administrative transfer	Commitment limited to length of sentence; parole rights preserved
West Virginia	Administrative transfer	Not specified
Wisconsin	Administrative transfer	Civil commitment proceedings required at end of sentence
Wyoming	Administrative transfer	Not specified
Federal	Administrative transfer	Commitment may not extend past end of prison term
District of Columbia	Administrative transfer	Not specified

Notes: Alabama has two separate provisions. One authorizes commitment to state mental hospitals through a court proceeding. The other allows administrative transfer to psychiatric facilities within the corrections department. Neither says specifically what happens to the prisoner when his term expires.

Idaho has two administrative transfer provisions. One allows prisoners to be hospitalized in state mental hospitals; the other allows transfer to a special institution for dangerously mentally ill persons and prisoners, which is to be maintained at Idaho State Penitentiary, but operated separately from the prison. (Other mental patients may be placed in this facility by court order.) Neither of these provisions indicates what is done with hospitalized prisoners whose terms have expired.

New York's statutes apply to commitment to Dannemora and Matteawan hospitals, which are maintained by the corrections department. Commitment is by a court proceeding, and is limited to six months, with two-year extensions allowed by court order.

Pennsylvania statutes provide for administrative transfer and also for judicial commitment of prisoners. Both these statutes require judicial commitment proceedings at the end of the prisoner's sentence.

years to life. In 1941, while he was in Clinton State Prison in New York, the prisoner began asserting that prison officials were corrupt. On the strength of a prison doctor's finding that Schuster had paranoid delusions of persecution by prison officials, he was transferred within twenty-four hours to Dannemora Hospital, one of the mental institutions operated by the New York Department of Corrections. He was still there when his petition for habeas corpus reached the court of appeals, more than twenty years after he would have been eligible for parole. Despite his repeated attempts to gain release, the issue of his mental state had never been decided by a court. At a 1963 hearing on a petition for habeas corpus, a psychiatrist testified that his only symptom was his "paranoid" delusions of prison corruption. At least some evidence of corruption was demonstrated by the fact that the warden, chief clerk, and controller of the prison had been dismissed shortly after the prisoner made his original charges.

Schuster was seeking to be returned to Clinton Prison for two reasons: he would be eligible for parole, and he would be removed from the atmosphere of Dannemora.

The state characterized his transfer to the hospital as nothing more than a change in the type of custody, but the court found that it involved basic rights. "Not only did the transfer effectively eliminate the possibility of Schuster's parole, but it significantly increased the restraints upon him, exposed him to extraordinary hardships, and caused him to suffer indignities, frustrations and dangers, both physical and psychological, he would not be required to endure in a typical prison setting."[2] The court noted examples of patients being "lost" in hospitals, stating, "Moreover, the facts reveal that there always lurks the grisly possibility that a prisoner placed in Dannemora will be marooned and forsaken."[3] The court continued, "Moreover, there is considerable evidence that a prolonged commitment in an institution providing only custodial confinement for the 'mentally sick' and nothing more may itself cause serious psychological harm or exacerbate any pre-existing conditions . . . . In addition, by its very nature, confinement at an institution for the criminally insane is far more restrictive than at a prison."[4]

Included in the appendix to the case is a detailed table from another prisoner petition comparing conditions at Bridgewater Treatment Center with those at the Massachusetts State Prison at Walpole. Less serious complaints include: free time was more closely regimented in the treatment center, fewer recreational activities were provided, canteen purchases were expensive and slow in arriving, magazines available to inmates were censored, and clothing was ill-fitting, limited in styles and quantities and only infrequently replaced with clean laundry. More serious problems included an inadequate number of toilets and showers, lack of privacy in visits with attorneys, and delays in outgoing mail, which was marked with a censor's stamp, and, if it went to a public official, accompanied by a letter of apology from the hospital staff.

The court held that prisoners were entitled to a hearing with substantially all the safeguards of a civil commitment proceeding before transfer to a hospital. It also ordered that Schuster be given a sanity hearing within sixty days.

In 1975 Schuster's case reached the same court again; because of a series of delays and objections by the state of New York, he was still in prison. The court characterized these delays as "flagrant violation of the spirit of our mandate." It ordered his unconditional release, saying that he should be considered to have been on constructive parole since 1969, and to have satisfied conditions qualifying him for absolute discharge.[5]

Matthews v. *Hardy*, 420 F.2d 607 (D.C. Cir., 1969), cert. den., 397 U.S. 1010 (1970), involved a prisoner serving a four-to-fourteen-year sentence for manslaughter at Lorton Reformatory in the District of Columbia. In March 1967, after serving two years, Matthews was certified as mentally ill and transferred to St. Elizabeths Hospital under 24 D.C. Code 302. He was returned to Lorton in August 1967. He alleged in his complaint that the transfer was unconstitutional because no judicial hearing was afforded, and he asked that prison officials be enjoined from further administrative transfers.

The government argued that administrative transfer was acceptable since the statute in question applied to persons already in the legal custody of the government. The court disagreed:

Concededly the authorities could not transfer a prisoner to St. Elizabeths absent some finding of mental illness. As to persons generally, Congress has erected in the 1964 Civil Commitment Act a full system of procedural safeguards before such a finding can be made. The appropriate question here is whether incarceration in a mental hospital is sufficiently different from incarceration in a prison to require the same or similar safeguards.

We answer the question in the affirmative. We think that prisoner transfers to a mental hospital do require protective procedures at least similar to those provided in the 1964 Act. First, although regrettable, it is a fact that there is a stigma attached to the mentally ill which is different from that attached to the criminal class in general. Thus a prisoner transferred to St. Elizabeths might well be described as "twice cursed." *United States et rel. Schuster* v. *Herold* [Citation omitted].

Second, there are numerous restrictions and routines in a mental hospital which differ significantly from those in a prison. Since these restrictions and routines are designed to aid and protect the mentally ill, persons, even prisoners, who do not have need for such discipline should not be subjected to it. Third, there is a definite possibility that transfer to St. Elizabeths might result in a prisoner being incarcerated for a longer time than if he remained at Lorton. Appellees were unable to assure us that inmates residing in St. Elizabeths would be called for parole hearings and considered for release on parole.

Most important, however, we are concerned that a person mistakenly placed in a mental hospital might suffer severe emotional and psychic harm.[6]

The court quoted language from *Schuster* on this point: "In considering the problem posed we are faced with the obvious but terrifying possibility that the prisoner may not be mentally ill at all. Yet . . . he will be exposed to physical, emotional and general mental agony. Confined with those who are insane, told repeatedly that he too is insane and indeed treated as insane, it does not take much for a man to question his own sanity and in the end to succumb to some mental aberration. . . ."[7]

The court concluded: "We think the differences in the two types of incarceration are simply too great to treat transfer to a mental hospital as a routine administrative procedure. The consequences of a mistake are sufficiently great to warrant giving prisoners the same protections as nonprisoners receive."[8]

The court then construed the District of Columbia statute to require that the prisoner be given a hearing, and, if requested, a jury trial, on the issue of mental illness, before he can be transferred to a mental hospital.

In *Baxstrom* v. *Herold*, 383 U.S. 107 (1966), the Supreme Court ruled that a prisoner who had been hospitalized as he was nearing the end of his prison term had been denied equal protection since he had not been granted a jury trial on the issue of mental illness, while all other persons committed to mental hospitals were entitled to such a trial. The court said:

Classification of mentally ill persons as either insane or dangerously insane of course may be a reasonable distinction for purposes of determining the type of custodial or medical care to be given, but it has no relevance whatever in the context of the opportunity to show whether a person is mentally ill *at all*. For purposes of granting judicial review before a jury of the question whether a person is mentally ill and in need of institutionalization, there is no conceivable basis for distinguishing the commitment of a person who is nearing the end of a penal term from all other civil commitments [Emphasis in original].[9]

The U.S. District Court for Northern West Virginia recently held that a prisoner may not be transferred to a mental hospital without the same procedural safeguards provided in civil commitments (*Sites* v. *McKenzie*, 423 F.Supp. 1190 (N.D.W.Va., 1976). The court also found unconstitutional, on equal protection grounds, state parole regulations denying parole consideration to these inmates until they recover.

Conclusions

Hospitalization of mentally disordered prison inmates has been thought of as a means of controlling and treating one class of "dangerous" offender. However, statutes providing for such transfers do very little to protect society from violent offenses. Prisoners who are mentally ill may be no more or less violent than others; further, the total number of mentally ill prisoners may be too small to be significant. The statutes discussed in this chapter reflect the view that the mentally ill are more violent than the rest of the population. Regardless of the degree of accuracy of this assumption, the statutes do not help in controlling violent offenders. Under the constitutional guidelines discussed above, statutes providing for hospitalization of prisoners cannot have the effect of extending their incarceration. These statutes may insure that a mentally ill prisoner gets the treatment he needs, but they do not offer any special benefit in dealing with violent offenders.

Notes

1. Code Ala. Tit. 15, Sec. 428; Ariz. Rev. Stat. 31-224, Ark. Stat. Ann. 59-415; Colo. Rev. Stat. 27-23-101; Conn. Gen. Stat. Ann. 17-194a; Del. Code Ann. Tit. 11, § 406, 6525; Fla. Stat. Ann. 945.12; Ga. Code Ann. 77-310; Hawaii Rev. Stat. 334-74; Idaho Code 66-335; Smith-Hurd Ill. Ann. Stat. Chap. 38, § 1003-8-5; Ind. Code 16-14-8-1 to 16-14-8-8; Iowa Code Ann. 783.5; Kan. Stat. Ann. 75-5209; Ky. Rev. Stat. Ann. 202.380; La. Stat. Ann. 28:59; Me. Rev. Stat. Ann. Chap. 34, §§136-A, 2333, 2333-A; Ann. Code Md. Art. 59, §16; Ann. Laws Mass. 123:18; Mich. Comp. Laws. Ann. 330.2000; Minn. Stat. Ann. 253.21; Vernon's Ann. Mo. Stat. 552.050; Rev. Stat. Neb. 305.03; Nev. Rev. Stat. 433.320; N.H. Rev. Stat. Ann. 651.10; N.J. Stat. Ann. 30:4-82; McKinney's N.Y. Corr. Law 383, 408; Gen. Stat. of N.C. 122-85; N.D. Century Code 12-47-27; Ohio Rev. Code 5125.05; Okla. Stat. Ann. Chap. 43A, §61; Purdon's Pa. Stat. Ann. Chap. 50, § 4411; Gen. Laws R.I. 26-4-6 to 26-4-9. Code Laws of S.C., 32-974; S.D. Comp. Laws 24-2-24; Vernon's Tex. Code Crim. 46.01; Utah Code Ann. 77-48-2; Vt. Stat. Ann. Tit. 28, § 703; Code Va. 19.2-177; W. Va. Code 28-5-31; Wis. Stat. Ann. 51-21; Wyo. Stat. 25-87; 18 U.S.C. 4241; 24 D.C. Code 302, 303.

2. 410 F.2d at 1078.

3. Ibid.

4. Ibid., at 1079, 1080.

5. *U.S. ex rel. Schuster* v. *Vincent*, 524 F.2d 153, 161 (2d Cir., 1975).

6. 420 F.2d at 610, 611.

7. Ibid., at 611.

8. Ibid.

9. 383 U.S. at 111, 112.

6

Mandatory Sentences and Miscellaneous Provisions

Introduction

This chapter is concerned with mandatory sentence statutes and miscellaneous statutes that may affect violent offenders. These include sex offender statutes, some of which require the registration of persons who have been convicted of sex offenses. Also included are some statutes limiting parole for cértain offenders, and others relating to psychiatric examination of prisoners before parole, commitment of ex-prisoners to mental hospitals, and similar statutes. As with some of the other statutes that have been discussed here, those in this group affect violent offenders quite unevenly. They include some nonviolent offenders and exclude some violent offenders. They are listed in this survey for two reasons: (1) mandatory sentence statutes are being proposed as an effective solution to crime problems, and it is the violent offender who seems to be the target of these proposals; and (2) the fact that state legislators have taken the time to enact one of the statutes in this chapter is an indication that they saw a special problem that needed to be dealt with. The statutes in this chapter thus may be regarded as an informal index of legislators' special concerns regarding crime in recent years.

The statutes have been divided into three groups: (1) mandatory sentences and limitations on probation or suspension of sentence; (2) sex offender statutes, including registration statutes; and (3) parole provisions, and all other miscellaneous statutes.

After a brief discussion of general characteristics of the group, each statute will be listed and described separately. The statutes in this chapter presented special research problems, since they are scattered throughout state codes, and it is difficult to find all of them. Therefore the chapter does not purport to be a comprehensive listing, but the statutes described should provide a useful picture of the approaches states have taken in recent years.

Mandatory Sentences and Parole Limitations

A mandatory sentence statute decreases the discretion a trial court may use in sentencing. Once the defendant has been convicted, the court is required to impose the sentence indicated in the statute and may not suspend it or decrease it below the specified length. This is in contrast to usual sentencing practices under which the court may exercise its general discretionary powers and suspend all or part of the sentence prescribed by law for a specific offense.[a]

A similar kind of statute prohibits the granting of probation or suspended sentences for a given offense. These laws do not affect the court's discretion to select any sentence within the range provided by statute (which may be very wide); once selected, however, the sentence may not be suspended. This means, in effect, that the offender must serve the minimum sentence authorized by law for the offense in question. Most of the commentary on mandatory sentencing is equally applicable to these probation statutes.

As James Vorenberg expressed it, "There are fashions in everything and today's fashion in criminal justice is the mandatory minimum sentence."[1] The enactment of such statutes has been an obvious response to the increasing volume of complaints from citizens and public officials alike that courts, with their great discretion in sentencing, are much too lenient, and that great numbers of crimes are committed by offenders who have been put "back on the street" after convictions. Vorenberg noted that both President Gerald Ford and Senator Edward M. Kennedy have proposed mandatory minimum sentences for federal crimes, but he also cited some reservations about the approach:

Simply adding mandatory minimum sentences to this situation will not make things better and may make them worse. There is a lot of experience in this country with such sentences, much of it bad. They have been used extensively for narcotics violations, yet recent newspaper reports indicate that drug traffic is at an all-time high.

When minimums are set very high, as they have been under Federal and state drug laws, some prosecutors, judges and juries evade the harsh results by not charging or by acquitting. The same thing can sometimes happen—and probably should—under low minimum statutes. One of the first people arrested under the Massachusetts gun law was a 73-year-old woman who was passing out religious leaflets from a paper bag in which she also kept a gun, presumably for self-protection. Her case was dismissed. Officials work hard to keep such people from spending a year in jail.

Even when prosecutors and judges do not think the statutory minimum is too high, they will evade the law and make their deals by finding an offense to charge that is not covered by the mandatory minimum sentence.

Burglars will be permitted to plead guilty to trespassing, muggers to assault and battery, and judges will sentence for these crimes. Prosecutors and judges will not do this because they want to, but because they must in order to buy enough guilty pleas to keep the flow of cases moving.[2]

A Boston trial lawyer, referring to the Massachusetts gun law, described another way to evade mandatory sentencing when he said, "Judges who had never before heard of the Constitution are now declaring searches to be illegal every time a gun is found in a white man's suit jacket."[3]

Despite some objections, mandatory sentencing bills are likely to be

---

[a]Some of the habitual criminal statutes discussed in Chapter 1 involve mandatory sentences for classes of offenses. Statutes listed here apply to specific offenses.

introduced in increasing numbers in state legislatures for at least several years to come. The following statutes are in effect:

Alaska. Persons sentenced under the Uniform Narcotic Drug Act may not be placed on probation until they have served a minimum term.[4]

Colorado. Probation is not permitted for class one felonies, class two petty offenses, or second or subsequent felonies.[5]

California. Suspension of sentences is not permitted for persons convicted of lewd and lascivious acts with children under ten unless the court has received a psychiatric report on the offender.[6]

Connecticut. For class A felonies (murder and first-degree kidnaping), the court must impose a minimum sentence of one year, with no reduction or suspension.[7]

Florida. No suspension or probation is permitted for repeat offenses, under the Uniform Narcotic Drug Act.[8]

Hawaii. Probation may not be granted for first- or second-degree murder, rape, carnal abuse of a female under twelve, incest between parent and child, arson, kidnaping, first-degree robbery, burglary when armed with a dangerous weapon, the giving or accepting of a bribe, or extortion by a public official.[9]

Indiana. Probation may not be granted for murder, arson, first-degree burglary, rape, treason, kidnaping, or a second robbery offense.[10]

Nevada. Probation may not be granted for first- or second-degree murder, forcible rape, or kidnaping.[11]

New York. An elaborate system of mandatory sentences is provided for the possession and sale of drugs. The penalties are as follows:

Class A felony—maximum, life; minimum set by court.

Class A-I felony—minimum between fifteen and twenty-five years.

Class A-II felony—minimum between six years and eight years, four months.

Class A-III felony—minimum between one year and eight years, four months.

Drug offenses are classified as follows:
A-I felony—sale of 1 oz of a narcotic drug or 2880 mg methadone; possession of 2 oz of a narcotic drug or 5760 mg methadone.

A-II felony—sale of 1/8 oz of a narcotic drug, 1/2 oz methamphetamine, 5 g of a stimulant, 5 mg LSD, 125 mg of a hallucinogen, 5 g of a hallucinogenic substance, or 360 mg methadone; possession of 1 oz of a narcotic drug, 2 oz methamphetamine, 10 g of a stimulant, 25 mg LSD, 625 mg of a hallucinogen, 25 g of a hallucinogenic substance, or 2880 mg methadone.

A-III felony—sale of a narcotic drug; sale of a stimulant, a hallucinogen, a hallucinogenic substance or LSD with a previous drug conviction; sale of 1 g of a stimulant, 1 mg LSD, 25 mg of a hallucinogen, 1 g of a hallucinogenic substance, or 1/8 oz methamphetamine; possession of a narcotic drug with intent to sell; possession of a stimulant, a hallucinogen, hallucinogenic substance or LSD with intent to sell and with a previous drug conviction; possession of 1 g of a stimulant, 1 mg LSD, 25 mg of a hallucinogen, 1 g of a hallucinogenic substance, or 1/8 oz methamphetamine with intent to sell; possession of 5 g of a stimulant, 5 mg LSD, 125 mg of a hallucinogen, or 5 g of a hallucinogenic substance.[12]

Ohio. Probation may not be granted for any offense committed while the offender is armed with a firearm or dangerous ordnance. In addition, probation may not be granted to any dangerous offender or repeat offender.[13] A repeat offender is defined to be "a person who has a history of persistent criminal activity, and whose character and condition reveal a substantial risk that he will commit another offense." A dangerous offender is "a person who has committed an offense, whose history, character, and condition reveal a substantial risk that he will be a danger to others, and whose conduct has been characterized by a pattern of repetitive, compulsive, or aggressive behavior with heedless indifference to the consequences."[14] "Dangerous offender" is defined to include, without limitation, psychopathic offenders, as defined in Ohio's sexual psychopath statute.[15]

Oregon. Mandatory sentences are imposed for any person who commits or attempts to commit a felony while armed with a pistol, revolver, machine gun, or other firearm capable of being concealed on the person, and who does not have a license to carry such a weapon. These sentences are to commence only on expiration of the sentence imposed for the offense committed while armed, and probation or suspended sentences may not be granted. The additional sentence is ten years for the first offense, fifteen years for the second, twenty-five years for the third, and a life term for the fourth.[16]

Pennsylvania. No probation may be granted for murder, kidnaping, poisoning, incest, sodomy, buggery, rape, assault and battery with intent to ravish, arson, robbery, or burglary.[17]

District of Columbia. Added sentences are imposed for the commission of a crime of violence while armed with a firearm or other deadly weapon.[b] The

[b]For purposes of this statute, crimes of violence are murder, manslaughter, rape, mayhem, maliciously disfiguring another, abduction, kidnaping, burglary, robbery, housebreaking,

sentence for the first such offense may be any term of imprisonment up to a life term. For a second armed offense, the offender must be sentenced to at least five years, with no suspension or probation allowed, and may be sentenced to any term up to life.[18]

Puerto Rico. Probation may not be granted for murder, robbery, incest, extortion, rape, infamous crime against nature, larceny, kidnaping, burglary, arson, or violations of the Puerto Rico Explosives Act.[19]

Sex Offender Statutes

The statutes in this group share some characteristics with the sexual psychopath statutes discussed in chapter 2. Most notably, they are applicable to some kinds of nonviolent or consensual behavior, and they probably are not enforced with any regularity or consistency. They are a further indication of the public's and the state legislatures' concern with sex offenses, particularly offenses involving children.

Alabama. Arrests and convictions of sex offenders are required to be reported by courts and arresting officers to the Department of Safety. This department is required to maintain records, which may be made available only to law enforcement officials. Failure to report an arrest or conviction is punishable by imprisonment.[20]

All persons convicted of sex offenses are required to register with the sheriff of their county of residence within thirty days of moving into the county. The sheriff must maintain records of these registrations, and he must also forward the information to the Department of Public Safety. Failure to register is punishable by a fine or imprisonment or both.[21]

The sex offenses included under both these provisions are crimes against nature; rape; carnal knowledge of a woman or girl; indecent molestation of children; indecent exposure; incest; pornography offenses; employing, harboring, or procuring prostitutes; using a girl aged ten to eighteen for prostitution or sexual intercourse; seduction; if a male, peeping into a room occupied by a female; or the attempt to commit any of these offenses.

California. Sex offenders are required to register with a sheriff or police chief within ten days of coming into any county or city. The record filed includes a written statement concerning the offense, and the offender's photograph and fingerprints.[22] If any person arrested for a sex offense is a teacher or school employee, law enforcement officers must notify the state teacher licensing board or school district officials.[23]

Offenses included under both these provisions are assault with intent to

---

larceny, assault with a dangerous weapon, or assault with intent to commit any of these offenses.

commit rape; sodomy; mayhem; robbery or grand larceny; inveigling or enticing an unmarried female under eighteen for prostitution; procuring by false pretenses; abduction of a female under eighteen for prostitution; seduction under promise of marriage; incest; lewd and lascivious act on a child under fourteen; oral copulation; or the attempt to commit any of these offenses. The two provisions also apply to any person declared to be a mentally disordered sex offender[24] and to any person convicted in another state of an act constituting one of the above offenses.

Florida. Under the Child Molester Act, courts have discretion either to commit persons convicted of sex offenses to Florida State Hospital for treatment and rehabilitation or to sentence them to a term not to exceed twenty-five years. Psychiatric examination is required before disposition. Offenses included are attempted rape, sodomy, attempted sodomy, crimes against nature, attempted crimes against nature, lewd and lascivious behavior, incest, attempted incest, and assault (when a sexual act is completed or attempted), when such acts are committed against, to, with, or in the presence of, a person fourteen years of age or younger.[25]

Georgia. Sixty days before parole or ninety days before the end of a prison term, the parole board may request mental examination and commitment proceedings for persons convicted of sex crimes.[26,c] The clerk of courts is required to keep records of all persons convicted of certain sex crimes.[d] The record must include name and alias, age, race, physical characteristics, nature of offense, previous sex offenses, previous offenses in the same county, permanent home address, and any other pertinent information.[27]

Maine. Wardens and superintendents of penal institutions are required to forward to the state police a copy of each sex offender's record and a statement of the facts of his case when the offender is paroled or discharged. Offenses included are indecent liberties with children, rape and carnal knowledge, carnal knowledge of a girl aged fourteen to sixteen, and assault with intent to rape.[28]

Michigan. Procedures are set out for prosecutions "for an offense committed by a sexually delinquent person for which may be imposed an alternate sentence to imprisonment for an indeterminate term, the minimum of which is one day and the maximum of which is life." Either the state or the defendant may introduce expert testimony; if the defendant pleads guilty, the court "shall conduct an examination of witnesses relative to the sexual delinquency of such person and

[c]Rape, assault with intent to rape, sodomy, kidnaping of a female by a male, incest, and molesting children to gratify a sex urge.

[d]Rape or attempted rape, molesting a minor, sodomy, bestiality, incest, kidnaping of a female by a male, soliciting for prostitution, and voyeurism.

may call on psychiatric and expert testimony." The only consequence of being declared a sexually delinquent person at the time of conviction, however, is that the testimony on sexual delinquency must be transcribed and placed in the court file, and that the court "may impose any punishment provided by law for such offense."[29]

A sexually delinquent person is defined as "any person whose sexual behavior is characterized by repetitive or compulsive acts which indicate a disregard of consequences or the recognized rights of others, or by the use of force upon another person in attempting sex relations of either a heterosexual or homosexual nature, or by commission of sexual aggressions against children under age 16."[30]

Nevada. Persons who have been convicted of sex offenses must register with the sheriff of their county of residence and must notify the sheriff of a change of address. The registration includes photograph, fingerprints, and a statement about the offense. Offenses included are assault with attempt to commit rape or the infamous crime against nature, forcible rape, statutory rape, incest, crime against nature, open or gross lewdness, lewdness with a child under fourteen, or an attempt to commit any of these offenses.[31]

South Dakota. Any person convicted of child molesting must be examined at a state mental hospital to ascertain if treatment is necessary. If the hospital superintendent finds the person to be mentally ill and amenable to hospitalization, "from the standpoint of his reasonably safe incarceration," that person shall be hospitalized as long as the superintendent finds treatment to be of medical value.[32]

Virginia. When a defendant is convicted of a crime that indicates sexual abnormality, the court, on its own motion or on motion of the prosecutor, defense counsel, defendant, or a person acting for the defendant, may defer sentence until a mental examination is made. The examination is conducted by the state department of mental health. A psychiatrist's report must be filed and must be made available to all parties to the case; the statute does not indicate what other use may be made of the report.[33]

Washington. Courts are authorized by statute to order the sterilization of any person convicted of rape or of carnal abuse of a female under the age of ten. This statute also applies to any person adjudged a habitual criminal.[34]

Parole Provisions and Miscellaneous Statutes

Limitations on parole give added information on offenses—or offenders—regarded as especially threatening by legislators and by the public. Especially interesting are the definition of "dangerously mentally ill person" (Idaho) and the provision for ex-convicts with "homicidal tendencies" (North Carolina). These statutes do not significantly expand the power of the state to confine or treat the persons described; however, legislators have been sufficiently concerned to enact the statutes. Presumably both they and their constituents feel safer with such laws on the books.

Delaware. A prisoner serving a sentence for a specified offense[e] may be paroled only after the parole board "has considered psychiatric and clinical studies of such person and is satisfied that he is free of any tendency to commit again the crime for which he was committed, or to violate any other law of this State." The statute requires clinical evaluation for at least thirty days within the five months immediately preceding release on parole.[35]

District of Columbia. The pretrial detention act was passed in July 1970; the statute was declared constitutional in *Blunt* v. *U.S.*[36] The statute includes a detailed description of the conditions under which a defendant may be denied pretrial release for reasons other than ensuring his appearance at trial. The statute refers to both "dangerous crimes" and "crimes of violence." A "dangerous crime" is defined to include "(A) taking or attempting to take property from another by force or threat of force, (B) unlawfully entering or attempting to enter any premises adaptable for overnight accommodation of persons or for carrying on business, (D) forcible rape, or assault with intent to commit forcible rape, or (E) unlawful sale or distribution of a narcotic or depressant or stimulant drug (as defined by any Act of Congress) if the offense is punishable by imprisonment for more than one year."[37] "Crime of violence" is defined to include murder; forcible rape; carnal knowledge of a female under sixteen; taking or attempting to take immoral, improper, or indecent liberties with a child under sixteen; mayhem; kidnaping; robbery; burglary; voluntary manslaughter; extortion or blackmail accompanied by threats of violence; arson; assault with a dangerous weapon; or an attempt or conspiracy to commit any of the foregoing offenses as defined by any act of Congress or any state law, if the offense is punishable by imprisonment for more than one year.[38]

The statute authorizes pretrial detention for the following three kinds of defendants:

1. A defendant charged with a dangerous crime, if the government certifies that based on the person's "past and present conduct" no set of conditions will reasonably assure the community's safety.

[e]Offenses included are murder; voluntary manslaughter; rape; kidnaping; abducting a child; poisoning with intent to harm; robbery; first- or second-degree burglary; mayhem; arson; assault with intent to commit murder, rape, or robbery; and the attempt to commit any of these offenses.

2. A defendant charged with a crime of violence, if the person has been convicted of a crime of violence within the preceding ten years, or if the crime presently charged was allegedly committed while the person was, with respect to another crime of violence, on bail, parole, probation or mandatory release pending completion of a sentence.

3. A person charged with any offense if, for the purpose of obstructing or attempting to obstruct justice, the person threatens, injures, intimidates, or attempts to threaten, injure, or intimidate any prospective witness or juror.

Before ordering pretrial detention, the court must hold a hearing and must find by clear and convincing evidence that the defendant falls within one of those three categories. In addition, for the first two categories, the court must find that there is a substantial probability that the defendant committed the offense with which he is charged. If the court orders pretrial detention, it must issue an order of detention accompanied by findings of fact and the reasons for its decision.

A defendant is entitled to be represented by counsel at the detention hearing, and he is entitled to present evidence or to testify, and to present witnesses in his own behalf. Information presented at the hearing need not conform to the rules of evidence. The defendant's testimony in the hearing is admissible only in proceedings involving failure to appear, offenses committed during release, violation of conditions of release, and perjury proceedings, and for purposes of impeachment of subsequent testimony. The defendant has the right to appeal an order of pretrial detention.

Defendants detained pending trial are entitled to have their cases placed on an expedited trial calendar. They are entitled to pretrial release if their trials have not begun within sixty calendar days (unless they have requested delays), or when a judicial officer finds that the basis for the detention no longer exists.

The statute also authorizes the pretrial detention of drug addicts charged with crimes of violence after medical examination, if the court, in a hearing, finds clear and convincing evidence that the defendant is an addict, finds a substantial probability that the defendant committed the offense charged, and finds that there is no condition or combination of conditions of release that will reasonably assure the safety of any other person or of the community.[39]

Idaho. A "dangerously mentally ill person" is defined to be a person found by a court "pursuant to any lawful proceeding" to be in such mental condition that he is in need of supervision, evaluation, treatment, and care; that he presents a substantial risk of harm to others as manifested by homicidal or other violent behavior or by evidence that others are placed in reasonable fear of violent behavior and serious physical harm; and that he is dangerous to such a degree that a more secure custodial facility is required than that deemed appropriate for most involuntarily committed mentally ill persons. Dangerously mentally ill persons may be committed to a mental institution maintained on the grounds of the Idaho State Penitentiary but operated separately from the prison.[40]

The following parole limitations are imposed by statute:

1. Offenders serving life sentences are eligible for parole only after they have served ten years.
2. Certain offenders may be paroled only "upon the examination or recommendation of one or more psychiatrists . . . to be selected by the state board of correction." This provision applies to those serving sentences for rape, incest, crime against nature, or committing a lewd act upon a child, or for attempt at any of these offenses, or for assault with intent to commit any of these offenses. It also applies to any prisoner "whose history and conduct indicate to the state board of correction that he is a sexually dangerous person." The term "sexually dangerous person" is not defined by statute.
3. Parole is not permitted for offenders sentenced for first- or second-degree murder where the victim was killed in the commission of a sex offense or in an attempt to commit a sex offense.
4. Parole is allowed only after five years or one-third of the sentence, whichever is less, for persons convicted of crimes of violence[f] or serving life sentences.[41]

Indiana. Certain drug users convicted of offenses are allowed to elect treatment under the supervision of the Department of Mental Health, instead of being sentenced to prison.[42]

Michigan. No parole may be granted before two years have been served for murder, forcible rape, armed robbery, kidnaping, extortion, or breaking and entering an occupied dwelling during the night, unless the time remaining to be served is less than two years.[43]

Mississippi. No person "whose records show him to be a confirmed and habitual criminal" may be paroled. No person convicted of a sex crime may be released on parole until he has been examined by a psychiatrist selected by the parole board and found to be of "normal and sound mind."[44]

North Carolina. "Whenever any person who has been confined in the State prison under sentence for the felonious killing of another person, and who has been discharged therefore at the expiration of his term of sentence, or as the

---

[f]Homicide in any degree, treason, rape where violence is an element of the crime, robbery of any kind, kidnaping, burglary when armed with a dangerous weapon, assault with intent to kill, murder in the second degree, rape, incest, crime against nature, committing a lewd act upon a child, attempt to commit any of these offenses, or assault with intent to commit any of these offenses.

result of executive clemency, shall thereafter so act as to justify the belief that he is possessed of a homicidal tendency, and shall be duly adjudged mentally ill [under commitment statutes], the clerk of the superior court or other officer having jurisdiction of the proceedings in which such person shall be adjudged mentally ill may, in his discretion, commit such person to [any state mental health facility]."[45]

Washington. The following minimums must be set by the board of prison terms and paroles, as time actually to be served:

1. first offenders armed with deadly weapons—at least five years
2. repeat offenders armed with deadly weapons at the time of the present offense—at least seven and one-half years
3. persons under life sentences as habitual criminals—fifteen years
4. persons convicted of embezzling from institutions of public deposit of which they were officers or stockholders—at least five years

These minimums may be reduced only for "meritorious effort in rehabilitation" and only on the vote of four members of the board.[46]

Conclusions

These statutes represent varying responses to specific crime problems, and also to specific public fears. Some of them increase the length of sentences served by certain offenders; others, such as sex offender registration statutes, purport to increase police efficiency through better record-keeping. Still others do little more than establish a label that has no real legal effect.

Like other statutes in this survey, many of these laws do not make careful distinctions between violent and nonviolent offenses. Instead, they single out sex offenses, firearm offenses, and drug offenses for special attention. They may or may not be useful in dealing with the specific problems they address; however, they do not appear to offer any special benefit in identifying or controlling violent offenders.

Notes

1. James Vorenberg, "Mandatory Sentence Becoming Fashionable," *Criminal Justice Digest* 4, no. 1 (January 1976): 4. Reprinted by permission of *Criminal Justice Digest*.

2. Ibid., pp. 5, 6.

3. Quoted in Alan Dershowitz, "Let the Punishment Fit the Crime," *New*

York Times Magazine, Dec. 21, 1975, pp. 7, 27. © 1975 by the New York Times Company. Reprinted by permission.

4. Alas. Stat. 17.10.200.

5. Colo. Rev. Stat. 16-11-201.

6. West's Cal. Pen. Code 288.1.

7. Conn. Gen. Stat. Ann. 53a-29.

8. West's Fla. Stat. Ann. 398.22.

9. Hawaii Rev. Stat. 711-77.

10. Ind. Code 35-7-1-1.

11. Nev. Rev. Stat. 176.185.

12. McKinney's N.Y. Pen. Code 60.00, 70.00, 220.16 to 220.43. See Pub. Health Law 3302 for schedules of controlled substances.

13. Ohio Rev. Code 2951.02.

14. Ohio Rev. Code 2929.01.

15. See chapter 2.

16. Ore. Rev. Stat. 166.230.

17. Purdon's Pa. Stat. Ann. Chap. 19, Sec. 1051.

18. 22 D.C. Code 3202.

19. Laws P.R. Ann. 34-1027.

20. Code of Ala. Tit. 15, §§ 443 to 447.

21. Ibid., §§ 448-456.

22. West's Cal. Pen. Code 290, 290.5

23. West's Cal. Pen. Code 291.

24. See chapter 2 on sexual psychopath statutes.

25. Fla. Stat. Ann. 801.11 *et seq.*

26. Ga. Code Ann. 77-539.

27. Ga. Code Ann. 24-2715.

28. Me. Rev. Stat. Ann. Chap. 34, § 1679.

29. Mich. Comp. Laws Ann. 767.61a.

30. Mich. Comp. Laws Ann. 750.10a.

31. Nev. Rev. Stat. 207.151 to 207.157.

32. S.D. Comp. Laws 22-22-9, 22-22-10.

33. Code of Va. 19.2-300.

34. Rev. Code Wash. Ann. 9.92.100.

35. Del. Code Ann. Tit. 11, Sec. 4353.

36. D.C. Ct. App. July 8, 1974, 15 Cr. L. Rptr. 2325.

37. 23 D.C. Code 1331 (3).

38. 23 D.C. Code 1331 (4).
39. 23 D.C. Code 1322-1332.
40. Idaho Code 66-361 to 66-363.
41. Idaho Code 20-233.
42. Ind. Code 16-13-7.5-15.
43. Mich. Comp. Laws Ann. 791.242.
44. Miss. Code Ann. 47-7-3.
45. Gen. Stat. N.C. 122-88.
46. Rev. Code Wash. Ann. 9.95.040.

7

Conclusions and Recommendations

Now that several kinds of statutes applicable to violent offenders have been described and discussed, general conclusions must be drawn about the function they serve in controlling violent crime, and suggestions should be made for improving upon them. At the outset, the problem is that these statutes do not represent any coherent, organized plan for dealing with violent offenders. Rather, they are a patchwork effort, pieced together over long periods, in varying social and political environments, and from different and sometimes conflicting perspectives. One can see progressive and humanitarian motives operating with vindictive public attitudes in the same statutes. Classical criminological ideas of inflicting punishment according to the seriousness of the offense struggle against theories characterizing offenders as defective people who must be isolated and restrained for society's protection. Some statutes appear to have resulted from hopes for scientific approaches and also from political exploitation of public fears of crime. Clinical perspectives have been grafted onto traditional legal principles to produce statutes whose purposes are not clear. Constitutional questions turn on the value of diagnoses and treatments that are the subjects of wide-ranging professional debate.

The statutes discussed in this book operate with numerous other statutes, which define offenses and set penalties, govern criminal procedure, establish corrections departments and parole boards, provide mental health services, authorize involuntary hospitalization and outline the powers of juvenile courts. Case law, administrative regulations, bureaucratic procedures, and the day-to-day decisions of prosecutors, prison officials, parole boards, and staffs of mental institutions—all are part of the law dealing with violent offenders.

In considering the conclusions, it is necessary to address a number of questions about present statutes and future proposals. In the preceding chapters the usefulness of the statutes in dealing with violent offenders, their constitutionality, and their ethical acceptability have been evaluated. Most of the statutes surveyed are not particularly useful in providing means to control violent offenders. But how are they lacking, and why were they not drafted in more effective terms?

Before making proposals for future statutes, principles will be described that must be followed so that violent offenders may be treated efficiently, sensibly, and justly. From these principles, some specific proposals for drafting of statutes can be derived.

An important question is whether there is a need for a special set of statutes

155

directed specifically toward the violent offender. Another is how much the drafting of statutes can reasonably be expected to accomplish in controlling violent offenders, and how much must be left to better protection of citizens, more efficiency in apprehending and convicting offenders, and more reasonable public attitudes toward "street crime."

Proposals for future statutes will include some discussion of a general approach to sentencing and of the goals that are properly adopted in sentencing and corrections, as well as a design for a better statutory approach to dangerous offenders.

A number of social and political factors have contributed to the current statutes. The one that seems most obvious is the association of mental illness and dangerousness. Not only do public attitudes support this association, but certain legal limitations give it added strength. The law is comfortable with the idea that mentally ill people may be confined for preventive and therapeutic purposes; however, it is not comfortable with the idea of such confinement for other persons. Therefore a person believed to pose a great risk of physical harm to others but not diagnosed as mentally ill could not legally or constitutionally be confined except after conviction for a specific offense, and subject to statutory limits on the length of the sentence. The same person, if diagnosed as mentally ill, could be confined for an indefinite period under a civil commitment statute or a sexual psychopath law. The need for a diagnosis of mental illness to deal with a particular person outside the present limits of the criminal law may have led to increased emphasis on the association between dangerousness and mental illness. The recent prominence of the therapeutic approach in criminology and corrections has had the same effect of suggesting that criminals, particularly violent offenders, must have an illness and must be amenable to cure. The result for the legal system has been a great deal of subterfuge and hypocrisy in devising quasi-criminal laws such as sexual psychopath statutes.

Another factor leading to present statutes is the preoccupation with sex offenders that has been prominent in U.S. legislative action during most of the time since the passage of the early sexual psychopath laws in the late 1930s. Because of this preoccupation, great amounts of public funds can be devoted to the commitment and treatment of an offender charged with such a minor crime as indecent exposure. In light of the serious problems confronting the criminal justice system, such an allocation of resources is intolerably wasteful.

The other major factor affecting the statutes' nature is the continuing tension between the traditional legal approach and the therapeutic approach. This division in criminology can be traced at least as far back as the eighteenth- and nineteenth-century debates over free will and determinism; in recent years in the United States the confusion between the two types of goals and methods has been apparent in much of the public debate over criminal justice and corrections. The tension seems particularly obvious in some of the statutes surveyed here.

The traditional punitive approach, now enjoying a new popularity under the label of "justice model" or "desert model," assumes that criminals commit crimes through choice; it takes as its goals punishment, deterrence, and to some extent, incapacitation. The therapeutic approach or clinical perspective assumes that tendencies to commit antisocial acts are defects that can be remedied by various forms of "treatment" or "rehabilitation." It accepts the necessity or desirability of incapacitation, if only until behavior can be changed through therapy. A number of characteristics of each model are particularly important in considering statutes concerning the dangerous offender.

The punitive model, deeply embedded in Anglo-American legal principles, concentrates on historical factual determinations: Did a particular act occur? Who did it? Was the actor legally culpable at the time? Were there provoking or mitigating circumstances? Such historical determinations, of course, are the kind our legal system feels most comfortable with. The therapeutic approach, on the other hand, concentrates less on the past and more on the future; it shows much less hesitancy to enter the field of prediction and address a different kind of question: Will a person be likely to commit undesirable acts in the future? Under what circumstances might such acts take place? What kinds of restrictions or interventions could prevent them?

Another way of looking at the two models is to say that the punitive model concentrates on the act committed, while the therapeutic approach concentrates on the actor. This emphasis on the individual is another area that the law has been reluctant to enter. There is no legal tradition to guide it in decisions focusing on individual characteristics, propensities, desires and motivations, as opposed to rules very generally governing human conduct and making no allowances for individual differences.

Numerous other philosophical distinctions could be made, of course, between the two approaches; however, some of the practical ones are more important to a consideration of statutes. The effect of the punitive model is frequently a shift toward very long sentences, particularly with respect to violent offenses, and it is apparent in habitual criminal statutes and mandatory sentencing laws. Even if a strict consideration of desert does not lead to a harsh result, the elements of incapacitation or deterrence are likely to do so, at least in the present social and political atmosphere. Such statutes may be attended by factors that mitigate the harsh effect in some cases: prosecutorial discretion not to charge the offense most strongly indicated, unwillingness of juries to convict or of courts to sentence, and the like. Ultimately such statutes may be applied only rarely, arbitrarily, or discriminatorily.

On the other hand, the effect of the therapeutic approach is often to increase the amount of discretion written into the statute, producing the kind of vagueness that is frequent in sexual psychopath laws. This is a formal, legally sanctioned discretion, as opposed to the informal, or even underground, kind of discretion often occurring under traditional legal standards. The therapeutic approach also allows discretion to be exercised by medical or psychological professionals working without clearly articulated standards, rather than by the traditional legal decision-making agencies. The other major effect is to abandon the principle of proportionality between the seriousness of the offense and the degree of the sanction opposed. (Punitive models may abandon proportionality in practice, but usually give more lip service to the idea.)

These factors have combined to create a set of statutes that promise a great deal for the control of violent offenders but deliver much less. Not only do they leave the problem of the violent offender unsolved, but they also create new problems in the fair and efficient administration of justice. What follows is a summary of objections to the statutes in this survey.

1. The statutes abandon the principle of proportionality. Laws such as sexual psychopath statutes and habitual criminal statutes do not distinguish violent offenses from nonviolent ones, or serious offenses from relatively unimportant ones, and many such statutes allow the same kinds of punishment or intervention for trivial offenses as for very serious ones.

2. Many of the statutes are hopelessly vague, especially the sexual psychopath statutes, which authorize long periods of incarceration and treatment for a class of offenders defined in almost meaningless terms. The amount of discretion written into many of the statutes is so great as to grant excessive power to the officials who interpret definitions or make decisions on confinement and release. This, of course, leads to great inconsistency in applying the statutes, and it opens the way for discriminatory application. In fact, one might argue that when a statute is written as vaguely as some of the sexual psychopath definitions, discrimination is almost required since it is nearly impossible to determine which offenders the statute is intended to include.

3. The statutes confuse the goals of punishment, incapacitation, and therapy. Some sexual psychopath statutes provide that treatment need not be provided unless resources are available, or unless an effective treatment exists (which often is not the case); the result is that the effects are punitive and incapacitative. But certain elements of these statutes—such as indeterminate commitments—are justified only on the ground that they are therapeutic and not punitive; if they were punitive, much shorter limits would be placed on the length of institutionalization. Similar logical conflicts are produced by sexual psychopath statutes that permit the offender to be returned to court for possible commitment to prison on a criminal sentence after he has been discharged from a mental institution as cured of his illness or abnormality. The offender may get the worst of both the punitive and the therapeutic worlds, as the Supreme Court noted that a juvenile offender might. He may be subjected to confinement in a secure institution for a longer period than would be permitted under strict criminal law standards and with fewer due process protections; yet he may not receive the therapeutic benefits promised by the medical model.

4. Many statutes allow—or require—discretion to be exercised by medical

professionals rather than by public policy-making agencies. It may be difficult or even impossible to determine the exact basis for such professional decisions if offenders wish to challenge them. Diagnoses of sexual psychopathy, defective delinquency, and the like may rest on a medical professional's assumptions that are never articulated or tested. Mental hospital superintendents charged with deciding when sexual psychopaths are no longer "too dangerous" to be released to the community may operate on entirely different guidelines from those that legislators intended in drafting the statute or courts would impose in interpreting it.

5. A number of the statutes rely heavily on assessments of personality traits and the prediction of violent behavior. These statutes seem to assume that such behavior can be predicted, in spite of the volume of literature pointing out the impossibility of making accurate predictions, the difficulties of overprediction, and the frequent lack of follow-up to determine whether predictions were correct. In addition to these basic problems with prediction, it is necessary to consider the fact that our legal system has little tradition in such decisions and has offered little guidance or limitation on the subject of predictive decisions. Courts tend to assume that while information appropriately considered for historical fact-finding must be carefully limited to prevent prejudice and discrimination and must be subject to challenge and careful testing to prevent errors, information considered in predictive decision-making need not meet such requirements. The result is that evidence such as hearsay, which would never be allowed in historical fact-finding, is routinely accepted in predictive determinations. The admission of such evidence can serve only to compound the difficulties already inherent in any attempt to predict human behavior.

6. The statutes generally do not assign intelligent priorities for the use of public resources. They allow great amounts of time, money, and effort to be devoted to prosecution, institutionalization, and treatment of persons charged with minor offenses at a time when serious offenses demand more and more attention. In view of public concern about serious crime, and in view of the undeniably high rates of serious crime, such statutes can be only counterproductive.

7. Penalties imposed under some of the statutes are so severe that police, courts, and juries may be unwilling to apply them as they stand; they may be completely ignored in most cases, or they may be used only as threats in plea-bargaining. This is most likely to be true of mandatory sentencing laws and habitual criminal laws with long mandatory sentences. General disuse of such laws, along with the singling out of a few offenders for severe penalties, and official overreaching in plea-bargaining, can serve only to erode respect for the law and for the functioning of the criminal justice system.

No criminal justice system can eliminate violent crime, particularly in a society as diverse, as mobile, as historically oriented to violence, and as individualistic as the United States. Not even by adopting the most oppressive approaches to identifying, punishing, treating, or incapacitating violent offenders could we eliminate serious offenses against the person and achieve the often-cited goal of streets where everyone can walk safely at all hours. Therefore we must think how we may best draft our statutes and arrange our criminal justice system to reduce the most serious and threatening kinds of crime without passing the point of diminishing returns where the inroads of the criminal justice system on personal freedom outweigh the benefits in personal safety. Many statutes in this survey are applied rarely and inconsistently; many laws that purport to be therapeutic do not provide effective therapy, or even any therapy at all; the offenses they seek to prevent are in many instances not serious; the laws include a number of oppressive elements, and there does not seem to be substantial agreement on the diagnosis or treatment of such conditions as "psychopathy" and "sociopathy." The benefits conferred on society—or on offenders—are much too doubtful to justify the statutes in their present form.

Better statutes can be drafted, however, by following the principle that efforts to protect society from violent offenders must also maintain and foster justice and fairness. Statutes that apply to violent offenders must promote respect for the law; they must respect and protect the rights of persons who are the subjects of legal proceedings under them, and they must avoid sanctions or interventions based on behavior that has not yet happened and may never happen. The following are necessary to promote these goals.

1. Elimination of preventive detention. Sanctions or interventions must be based on past behavior rather than on predictions or personality characteristics.
2. Punishment as the justification for sanctions for criminal behavior. While other goals, such as rehabilitation, deterrence, and incapacitation, may be served by criminal sanctions, they are not sufficient to justify sanctions.
3. Proportionality. Any sanction or intervention must be proportioned to the seriousness of the harm caused by the offender. Proportionality implies careful distinctions between violent and nonviolent offenses and between serious and nonserious offenses; it also implies the setting of priorities so that public resources may be devoted primarily to the most serious offenses.
4. Protection of due process. In this context due process is taken to include not only procedural protections to safeguard the integrity and accuracy of decision-making, but also the restriction of decision-making powers to appropriate public policy agencies and the limitation of discretion.

Eliminating Preventive Detention

Whether predictions of violent behavior should ever be made the basis for state intervention is a complex question. Certainly a prediction of violence is not sufficient to justify intervention or incarceration when we know that many—and perhaps most—of such predictions are erroneous; it is clearly unjust to detain the "false positives" to restrain or treat the "true positives." Another difficulty arises from the already mentioned fact that traditional legal limitations on the kind of evidence allowed in historical determinations have not been imposed on predictive decisions. Courts apparently believe that a wider range of information should be available for such decisions than for other kinds of legal proceedings. The result has been that evidence such as hearsay has been used in predictive decisions, with consequent possibilities of prejudice and bias through labeling.

Even if the evidentiary questions were to be settled, and even if a predictive method were available that could identify most of the people who would later engage in violence without overpredicting, some problems would remain. Is it just to detain, imprison, treat, or otherwise control a person on the basis of something he has not done yet? It is difficult to argue that a society must wait until an expected harm is done before intervening; on the other hand, there is something offensive about being detained or treated because of a predicted future act. (In fact, with a few exceptions, the criminal law does not punish persons who have intended harm but have not committed any act to bring it about.) A catch-22 is introduced: if a future act is the basis of the state's right to interfere, and if the interference prevents the act, then the basis for intervention has been eliminated. (Of course, one may argue that if the accurate predictive system described above were available, it might be possible to prevent many of the predicted harms by protecting the potential victims rather than detaining the prospective offender.)

For the present, it seems safe to say that the lack of ability to accurately predict violent behavior without overpredicting justifies opposition to interventions based on predictions.

There is not the slightest doubt that prediction enters strongly into almost every decision made in the criminal justice system. While it would be gross self-delusion to believe that predictive elements could ever be completely eliminated from such decision-making, it does seem possible to greatly reduce and narrowly restrict prediction, and to require that decisions on intervention have independent legal bases.

Punishment as Justification for Sanctions

Criminal offenders may be imprisoned, fined, or subjected to other restrictions on liberty for the purpose of punishment. Punishment is both a necessary and a sufficient justification for criminal sanctions. The goals of rehabilitation, deterrence, and incapacitation are not objectionable per se; however, our ability to achieve them within a just and humane system is open to serious question. Even if these goals could be fulfilled, they do not provide sufficient justification for criminal sanctions.

These secondary goals need not be abandoned in accepting punishment as the justification for a criminal justice system, although their scope will be limited. Some offenders will be deterred from future crimes by punishment; some will be incapacitated from committing additional crimes during the time of their punishment. While offenders are being punished, they may be educated, socialized, treated, and counseled. These are services provided to convicted offenders, however, not reasons for their imprisonment or punishment.

While the term "punishment" may have a harsh ring, following on so many years of praise for the idea of rehabilitation, punishment need not be harsh. The idea of punishment or desert operates not only as a justification for state intervention, but also as a limit; the concept of punishment implies the concept of proportionality.

Proportionality

The idea of proportionality is at least as old as the biblical injunction to take an eye for an eye and a tooth for a tooth. As an element of basic fairness it is strongly supported today by many who are concerned about disparities in sentencing; some of these people are learned jurists and others are prison inmates who complain that their sentences are longer than those of other prisoners who committed the same offense. Proportionality is usually considered necessary with respect to punishment; it also should apply to any other interventions based on offending behavior.

The therapeutic approach is necessarily in conflict with the principle of proportionality because it assumes that a treatment program should be tailored to individual characteristics and needs of offenders; it follows that one offender may "need" much more intensive or more extended treatment than another to produce the desired change. The two may have been selected for treatment because they committed the same kind of prohibited acts, but they are being treated for entirely different sets of underlying conditions or deficiencies. To abandon one offender's treatment before it is completed merely because others who engaged in the same kind of behavior have been successfully treated in a shorter time, or because of an absolute limit on the length or type of treatment, would seem illogical and self-defeating to one who accepts the premises of the therapeutic approach. Unfortunately, there are a number of problems with therapeutic purposes.

First, there are serious doubts that the promised benefits of treatment are actually forthcoming; without these benefits, the rationale for abandoning proportionality disappears. With respect to sexual psychopath statutes, arguments concerning unavailability and ineffectiveness of treatment seem especially strong. Since some of the statutes do not even require that treatment be provided in all cases—and some allow the subjects to be transferred to prisons—and since public resources for providing effective treatment are scarce in many of the states that have such laws, the results seem substantially less beneficial than the statutes' language would suggest. In fact, the Fourth Circuit Court of Appeals, in a series of cases upholding the constitutionality of the Maryland Defective Delinquent Act, admitted, even while praising the therapeutic ideal, that there are no known treatments for some of the people diagnosed as defective delinquents, and that for them the statute represents nothing more than authority for imprisoning them indefinitely, perhaps for life.[1] If this is true in Maryland, which has devoted more resources than most states to the diagnosis and treatment of "psychopathic offenders," one can hardly be optimistic about the benefits to be derived from statutes with therapeutic purposes.

Further, even the best-intentioned, best-managed, and most successful therapeutic programs are often regarded as punitive by persons subjected to them against their wills. This fact was recognized by the Supreme Court in *In re Gault,* 387 U.S. 1 (1966), in which Justice Abe Fortas's opinion said:

A boy is charged with misconduct. The boy is committed to an institution where he may be restrained of liberty for years. It is of no constitutional consequence— and of limited practical meaning—that the institution to which he is committed is called an Industrial School. The fact of the matter is that, however euphemistic the title, a "receiving home" or an "industrial school" for juveniles is an institution of confinement in which the child is incarcerated for a greater or lesser time. His world becomes "a building with whitewashed walls, regimented routine and institutional hours . . . ." Instead of mother and father and sisters and brothers and friends and classmates, his world is peopled by guards, custodians, state employees, and "delinquents" confined with him for anything from waywardness to rape and homicide.[2]

The same thing might perhaps be said of an institution for defective delinquents or a state hospital for the criminally insane. In fact, "humanitarian" schemes for "treating" rather than "punishing" offenders have been described as follows: "To be taken without consent from my home and friends; to lose my liberty; to undergo all those assaults on my personality which modern psychotherapy knows how to deliver; to be re-made after some pattern of 'normality' hatched in a Viennese laboratory to which I never professed allegiance; to know that this process will never end until either my captors have succeeded or I grow wise enough to cheat them with apparent success—who cares whether this is called Punishment or not?"[3]

The subjects of therapeutic programs, as well as the public, may regard those programs as part of the same punitive approach taken by traditional criminal sanctions. For example, in discussing application of the insanity defense in Ohio, a television news reporter recounted the case of a man charged with murder who had been acquitted on grounds of insanity and so "got off with only six months in a mental hospital." Although the treatment imposed was thought insufficient for the offense, it seemed to be considered punishment. It was not seen in the way the law describes it—treatment provided for a person not legally culpable.

Given the present widespread dissatisfaction with disparity in criminal sentencing, and the public's confusion between therapeutic and punitive approaches—a confusion, incidentally, that is reflected in the imprecise drafting of statutes in this survey—it follows that proportionality in dealing with offenders could do a great deal to increase respect for the law and trust in it.

Proportionality can also help to maintain the importance of human life and physical safety. When the law treats property offenses more severely than serious offenses against the person, or even equally severely, the importance of protecting human life and safety is demeaned.

Of course, proportionality in penalties for direct crimes against the person is not enough to restore trust in the law. As long as manufacturers of hazardous products, builders of firetrap apartments, companies that poison the environment and their own employees with highly toxic chemicals, and sellers of untested or unsafe drugs are punished with token fines and suspended jail sentences and then allowed to return to their dangerous practices, respect for justice will be lacking. As long as conspirators who steal millions from medical assistance programs for the needy and perpetrators of monolithic schemes to defraud the public and the government are considered too "respectable" to be imprisoned with "common criminals," there will be no overall proportionality in the criminal justice system. While the seriousness of these white-collar crimes should not be minimized, the changes proposed here are necessary because they can be the beginning of a more just and a more respected criminal law.

Further, proportionality between the seriousness of the offense and the degree of sanction is one way of setting priorities for expenditures of public resources. While it does not always cost less to prosecute or punish a minor offense with a minor penalty than to prosecute a very serious offense, limiting the most severe punishments and the most elaborate treatment or rehabilitation approaches to the most serious offenses will help bring about a better overall apportionment of resources. Some of the major cases on sexual psychopath statutes have concerned offenders convicted of indecent exposure, committed for indeterminate periods, and confined for several years. A society facing serious crime problems certainly cannot afford to use large amounts of the time of police, prosecutors, courts, and state institutions for such cases.

Proportionality is a concept that must be supported, both as a principle of justice and fairness, and as an approach that may provide substantial practical benefits.

Protection of Due Process

Due process implies a basic recognition of individual rights, and a basic respect for them that is often missing in therapeutic approaches. If one looks closely at almost any legal provision having to do with mentally disordered people, one can detect a suggestion that their rights are less important than those of "normal" people. The mentally ill are often explicitly excepted from discussions of the need to protect individual rights from any unauthorized encroachment by the state. It is only within the last twenty or twenty-five years that the lack of procedural protections in civil commitment proceedings has been seriously challenged, and most commitment statutes still provide substantially less in the way of due process than do criminal proceedings. Ours is a society in which criminal defendants and convicted criminals are regarded with a great deal of distaste, and the stigma of mental illness is strong enough to destroy job opportunities, family and social relationships, and political aspirations. Mentally disordered offenders are social discards. It is not surprising, then, that procedural protections have been notably lacking for offenders who fall into the Never-Never-Land between the criminal justice system and the mental health system.

Many sexual psychopath statutes do not address the means by which a person committed as a sexual psychopath may challenge the continued justification for his confinement. The Maryland statute, however, does address the issue, and solves it by stating specifically that the subject may not bring court action to test the validity of his continued institutionalization until he has been confined for two-thirds of his criminal sentence, or two years, whichever is greater; moreover, he may bring subsequent challenges only every three years. This does not mean, of course, that other remedies—such as petitions for writs of habeas corpus—are not available; it does mean, however, that drafters of such statutes have not been sensitive to the value of procedural protections.

Any decision-making process of the type required by the statutes in this survey will produce some errors. No scheme for dealing with violent offenders is justifiable unless it recognizes the inevitability of errors and provides procedures for correcting them.

This approach recognizes that the offender, whether considered mentally disordered or not, values his liberty and self-determination as much as anyone else and that society must accord them equal value as well. The question addressed must not be whether the state can articulate a reason for confining, punishing, or treating such an offender, but whether that reason outweighs the importance of the offender's liberty. The state must expect that subjects of such proceedings will seek to assert every defense available to prevent institutionalization and to use every legal tool available. It has not been uncommon for professional people to treat assertions of innocence or protests against confinement as symptoms of pathology that offer further proof that intervention is necessary.[4] Statutory schemes and the courts that administer them must not permit such assumptions to interfere with the respect due the subject's rights or with the procedures provided to protect them.

In practical terms, these considerations mean that the fact-finding process must be protected by careful limits on the kinds of evidence admitted, and by the right to challenge evidence, especially to explore the factual bases for conclusions of expert witnesses. Procedures must be provided for appeals and challenges to any decisions involving the liberty and self-determination of accused offenders.

Another equally important element of due process involves the issue of who should make the operative decisions on confining, punishing, or treating offenders. The distinction between medical or psychological decisions and public policy decisions has been blurred during the ascendancy of the therapeutic approach; however, it is one that must be maintained and strengthened. The description and diagnosis of mental disorders, the formulation and carrying out of treatment plans, and the decision about when a patient has improved to the point that therapy is no longer indicated are properly considered medical decisions. But the question of what kinds of conduct justify intervention by society, what degree of intrusion is justified, what kinds of therapy ought to be imposed against the will of the offender, and when release is appropriate are not medical decisions, but public policy decisions. They must be made by the same agencies that make and carry out other public policies: legislatures, courts, and juries.

Psychiatric testimony about an offender may be quite useful in making decisions concerning him; however, the fact that a psychiatrist thinks that the person needs therapy, or that a psychiatrist is willing to predict his future behavior, or that a treatment mode exists that may improve or eliminate the offending behavior is not relevant to the question of whether state intervention is justifiable.

Further, the distinction between diagnostic determinations and factual determinations about what a particular person has done must be maintained. Since medical and psychological professionals often base conclusions on assessments of the person's past behavior, and since the nature of this behavior may not have been established, it is important to determine the factual basis for medical conclusions.

This distinction between medical decisions and public policy decisions will not be easy to maintain; however, it is possible to devise procedures that will enable courts to use medical expertise without being overwhelmed by it or without abdicating their own responsibilities.

The principles outlined above suggest both a general approach to drafting better statutes and some specific recommendations.

Since violent offenses must be dealt with under the same legal principles that apply to other criminal sanctions, there is no need for a special body of statutes directed toward violent offenders. They could establish no special powers and would serve no real purpose. It is appropriate, however, in organizing statutes, to include a category of violent offenses, or of serious offenses against the person, as well as of other offenses against the person, offenses against property, offenses against public trust, and the like. Such distinctions help to emphasize the conceptual differences between aggravated assault or attempted murder on the one hand, and simple assault, threats, or larceny from the person on the other, as well as the difference between any of these offenses and simple theft, car theft, or forgery. Such categorizations, with penalties appropriately graded to the seriousness of the offense, can improve both the practical usefulness of the statutes in imposing fair and proportional punishments and the symbolic function of the law in reflecting societal limits on behavior and in assigning priorities to property values, human safety, and public order. More rationally drafted criminal codes will not solve the crime problem, and cannot, of themselves, make individual citizens safer in their daily activities. Of course, every problem cannot be solved by enacting a new statute. Other sectors of the criminal justice system must also be made more efficient if crime rates are to be decreased: police departments, court systems, corrections departments and probation and parole services, among others. But none of these efforts can be successful unless it is backed by criminal laws that clearly detail intolerable behavior, set priorities on the values that are injured by proscribed behavior, and establish penalties appropriate to those values. Such statutes are not sufficient to a rational criminal justice system, but they are a necessary part of it. Criminal codes ought to be revised to meet these standards, at the same time that other efforts are undertaken to improve the criminal justice system.

Sentencing should be in line with the proposals in Dershowitz's *"Fair and Certain Punishment"*;[5] it involves relatively short sentences carefully proportioned to the particular offense. Legislatures would fix the sentences, and courts would have the authority to vary the basic sentence by one-fourth to one-third, on the basis of aggravating or mitigating factors, which judges would be required to specify in imposing sentences. Some reduction in prison terms ought to be allowed for good behavior to provide incentives for orderly conduct within the institution. Short periods of parole supervision and services or similar re-entry programs ought to be available to decrease the difficulties faced by the newly released prisoner. (While experimentation with alternatives to imprisonment—such as restitution or public service work—should be encouraged, these approaches will not usually be appropriate for violent offenders.)

Information to be considered in sentencing should be limited to the events surrounding the offense, the offender's state of mind at the time of the offense, and the offender's previous convictions.

Recommendations

Organization of Statutes

1. There should be three categories of offenses against the person. The first would include violent offenses and offenses involving injuries to victims, such as aggravated assault, armed robbery, rape and other sexual assaults, manslaughter,

and attempted murder. The second would include offenses involving threats or risks of injury but no actual injury; these offenses might be robbery with no injury to the victim, kidnaping with no injury to the victim, extortion by threats of violence, and attempted rape. The final category would include any minor offenses against the person, such as interfering with the custody of a person under arrest, permitting a dangerous animal to be at large, and larceny from the person.

2. Penalties would not necessarily be the same for every offense within a category, but they would fall within the same range. Penalties for offenses against the person would not always be greater than penalties for offenses against property. For example, an offender who had devised and carried out an elaborate scheme of fraud against numerous victims might be punished as severely as one who had committed an assault or an armed robbery.

Sentencing

1. Sentences should be shorter than those imposed in most states today; further, some attention should be given to the question of whether more severe penalties make it more difficult to convict offenders.

2. Repeat offenders should be subject to a series of measured increases in sentences for each successive offense. A small increase with each offense is more fair and more rational than a drastic increase in penalty upon a specific number of offenses, as under present habitual criminal statutes. The added penalty should be calculated as a percentage of the sentence for the present offense; statutes drafted in this way can impose added punishment for persistent criminality, while avoiding the incongruity of sentences that are grossly out of proportion to the penalty for the present offense. Perhaps the simplest way of drafting this kind of statute would be to make the record of previous convictions one of the aggravating factors to be considered under general sentencing procedures.

3. Penalty plans should be drafted to offer offenders some incentive to choose a lesser offense over a greater one, when a choice presents itself. Attempts should be punished less severely than completed offenses; and the abandonment of criminal behavior after it has already begun should be rewarded with a lighter sentence. A robber who confronts a storeowner with a gun and then flees without taking any money, or a kidnaper who releases a victim in a short time instead of presenting a ransom demand should be subjected to less punishment than their counterparts who carry through their plans. Again, these gradations in penalties may be created by considering the abandonment of attempts as a mitigating factor in sentencing.

4. Aggravating and mitigating factors should be spelled out in very specific terms. For example, some current death penalty statutes include such aggravat-

ing factors as the fact that an offense was committed in an especially cruel or heinous fashion. It would be better to list such specific factors as the degree of injury, disability, or disfigurement suffered by the victim; the victim's age, physical condition, and degree of helplessness; the length of time over which injuries were inflicted, the length of time the victim was held prisoner, whether the victim was subjected to threats, and whether injuries were inflicted in circumstances where they did not contribute to the success of the crime or the offender's escape.

Expert Testimony

1. Expert testimony will generally be relevant only to questions of criminal responsibility under an insanity defense, and to mental state as a mitigating factor in sentencing. It should be admitted only concerning those issues, and limiting instructions should be given to juries so that it is not improperly considered.

2. Expert testimony should not be admitted until the expert witness has presented the factual basis for his opinion.

Treatment

1. For purposes of these recommendations, the term "treatment" includes not only such common procedures as psychoanalysis, group therapy, medical care for physical conditions, education, job training, family counseling and the like, but also more experimental modes such as behavior modification, aversive therapy, drug therapies, and other, yet undeveloped methods.

2. Treatment programs should be made available to offenders serving prison terms, either as community programs extended to prisoners or as special programs operated by prisons.

3. Prisoners should be allowed to participate in treatment programs entirely at their own option, provided that the programs can be carried out in a custodial setting and the prisoners understand what the treatment entails. The second requirement calls for a kind of informed consent, with the formality of the consent depending on the chosen treatment's complexity and risks.

4. For programs such as academic education and job training, it may be appropriate to permit a prisoner to participate only if he agrees to complete a specific course or period of treatment. These regulations, imposed for administrative convenience, would not apply to more intrusive therapies, which prisoners must be allowed to discontinue at any time.

5. Arrangements should be made for prisoners to continue treatment after their release if they wish to do so and if the directors of the treatment program believe that continued treatment can be of benefit.

6. No prisoner should be required to accept treatment unless a court orders it after finding the following:

a. The treatment can produce substantial benefits without the prisoner's cooperation and within the time the prisoner will be imprisoned.
b. The treatment must not cause any permanent impairment of physical or mental functions or create risks to life or health.
c. The treatment must not involve painful or highly unpleasant effects or unusual deprivations of privileges.

If involuntary treatment is ordered, the court must review the program frequently to determine that these guidelines continue to be met.

These changes in criminal codes cannot eliminate the threat of violent offenses; that result must await social, political, psychological, and technological advances that cannot be foreseen. But these recommendations should help to improve both the law applicable to violent offenders, and the practical, day-to-day operations of the criminal justice system as it relates to them. These changes should introduce a greater measure of fairness and should foster greater respect for the law. They should eliminate most of the objections to present statutes, and they should provide an intelligent framework for continuing attempts to deal with the very difficult problem of violent crimes.

Notes

1. See *Sas* v. *Maryland*, 334 F.2d 506, 513 (4th Cir., 1964).

2. 387 U.S. at 27.

3. C.S. Lewis, "The Humanitarian Theory of Punishment" 6 *Res Judicatae* 224, 227 (1953). Reprinted with permission.

4. See, e.g., *McNeil* v. *Director*, 407 U.S. 245 (1972).

5. *Report of the Twentieth Century Fund Task Force on Criminal Sentencing*, with background paper by Alan Dershowitz (New York: McGraw-Hill, 1976).

Table of Cases

Index

Index

appeal, 42, 73, 83, 165

Blackstone, William, 105
burden of proof, 25, 26, 71, 96-97, 100, 124

civil statutes, 62-64, 89-96, 98
commitment, 41, 45, 66, 69-70, 82, 84-100, 106, 111, 120, 121-124, 131-133
constitutionality of statutes, 20-21, 25-26, 42, 57, 84-100, 111, 114, 124-129, 133, 136-138
contempt, 97-98
criminal sexual deviant, 80-82
criminal statutes, 62-64, 89-96, 98
cruel and unusual punishment, 20-21, 84, 94-95

dangerousness
  association with mental illness, 22, 105, 131
  generally, 22-24, 26
  persons acquitted by reason of insanity, 119, 120, 121
  sexual psychopath statutes, 41, 45, 56, 57, 59, 86, 97
decision-making, 62, 66-69, 96-97, 122, 165, 166
defective delinquent, 56, 78, 79
Defective Delinquent Act, Maryland, 42, 57, 59, 75, 78-80, 83, 85-86, 90-93, 97-100, 165
definitions
  incompetence to stand trial, 105-110
  sexual psychopath statutes, 42, 45, 56-57, 85-89
Dershowitz, Alan, 62-64, 167
double jeopardy, 20, 84
drug offenses, 143-144
due process of law, 25, 42, 66, 84, 89, 92, 98, 99, 127, 136-138, 160
Durham rule, 119

equal protection, 20, 84, 85, 113, 128-129, 136-138
ethical acceptability of statutes, 26, 42, 100-101, 114
expert testimony, 69, 90-91, 127, 166, 169

habeas corpus, 73, 82, 89, 124
hearsay, 62, 71, 161
history, 1, 43-45

incapacitation, 1, 162
incompetence to stand trial, definition, 105-110
indictment, 89
insanity (lack of criminal responsibility), 57, 87-88, 106, 119-120

Katkin, Daniel, 18-19
Kittrie, Nicholas, 43

"labeling game," 62-64

medical model, 42
mental hospitals
  generally, 73, 81, 106
  secure hospitals (hospitals for the criminally insane), 73, 96, 106, 132
mental illness
  association with dangerousness, 22, 41, 44, 45, 56, 57, 87-88, 105, 119, 120, 121, 131
  generally, 41, 93, 106, 132
mental retardation, 43, 107, 111
Model Penal Code, 21, 22, 24; text, 33-34
Model Sentencing Act, 21, 24; text 35-36

parens patriae, 41
parole, 62, 64, 80, 131, 133, 138, 147-151
Patuxent Institution, 66, 73, 79, 83

175

About the Author

Linda Sleffel graduated Phi Beta Kappa from the William Allen White School of Journalism and Public Information of the University of Kansas. After working for three years as a copy editor for the *Topeka Daily Capital*, she returned to Kansas University and received a law degree in 1974. This book was prepared while Ms. Sleffel was working at the Academy for Contemporary Problems in Columbus, Ohio.